THE ULTIMATE **MIXER** COOKBOOK

THE ULTIMATE **MIXER** COOKBOOK

ROSEMARY MOON AND KATIE BISHOP

RUNNING PRESS

A QUINTET BOOK

Copyright © 2002 Quintet Publishing Limited
First published in the United States of America in 2002 by Running Press Book Publishers.

9 8 7 6 5 4 3 2 1
Digit on the right indicates the number of this printing
Library of Congress Cataloging-in-Publication Number 2002093013
ISBN 0-7624-1452-9

This book was designed and produced by Quintet Publishing Limited
6 Blundell Street
London N7 9BH

Editor: Erin Connell
Photography: Ian Garlick
Food Stylists: Emma Patmore and Jacqueline Bellefontaine
Designer: Janis Utton
Managing Editor: Diana Steedman
Creative Director: Richard Dewing
Publisher: Oliver Salzmann

KitchenAid® The shape of the mixer is a registered trademark of KitchenAid USA. All KitchenAid
trademarks used with permission. *The Ultimate Mixer Cookbook* was not produced by or sponsored
by KitchenAid USA.

This book may be ordered by mail from the publisher.
But try your bookstore first!

Running Press Book Publishers
125 South Twenty-second Street
Philadelphia, Pennsylvania 19103-4399
Visit us on the web!
www.runningpress.com

Manufactured in Singapore by Universal Graphics Pte Ltd
Printed in China by Leefung-Asco Printers Trading Ltd

WARNING   *Because of the slight risk of salmonella, raw eggs should not
be served to the very young, the ill or elderly, or to pregnant women.*

CONTENTS

INTRODUCTION

Time in the kitchen is at a premium these days – there is a balancing act to perform between working and running the household that results in home cooking too often becoming a casualty of the modern lifestyle.

We all know that homemade food not only tastes best and is nutritionally sound, being free of additives and preservatives, but that people love it. So, a kitchen assistant that can perform the most labor-intensive and repetitive jobs, giving you control of the creative side of cooking without having to worry about the time-consuming grind, is as helpful as an extra pair of hands when it comes to making home baked food for your family and friends.

A stand mixer does just that – it takes care of all the hard, time-consuming, and heavy jobs that deter so many people from enjoying the pleasures of cooking. Whether you cook for one, two, or a crowd, a mixer that will beat, stir, knead, and mix will make your life in the kitchen easier and far more pleasurable.

A MULTI-PURPOSE MIXER

Most people can cook when the recipe calls for heating a few ingredients together in a saucepan, or popping a store bought pie into the oven. However, the basic techniques of creaming, whisking, and kneading often defeat the home cook, or sound too time-consuming even to be attempted on a daily basis. These tasks, however, are the very essence of a mixer's role, as well as being the foundation of an accomplished cook's skills.

Admittedly, eating habits have changed dramatically over the last decade or so, and the pies and cakes of yesteryear are no longer on most day-to-day family menus. **KitchenAid**® stand mixers, and Kenwoods, are, however, much more than just mixers for baking. They can be used for mixing any large quantities of food, be it homemade burgers, mashed potatoes, or whisking mayonnaise or salad dressings. Leave your mixer out on the kitchen counter rather than storing it in a cupboard, and you will find more and more uses for it!

PLANETARY ACTION

The best modern stand mixers employ the most thorough mixing technique ever introduced for domestic food preparation machines – planetary action. This means the beater revolves constantly, while at the same time the hub in which the beater is located moves around the bowl. Thus, every single area of the bowl is reached, ensuring perfect mixing. Just occasionally, a mixture that is very sticky may need to be scraped down the sides of the bowl – this may happen only once or twice during any process.

PICK A COLOR, PICK A STYLE

Gone are the days when kitchen appliances came in only one color, that being white. Stand mixers are now available in a variety of shapes and sizes, and your budget might well dictate choice as much as color scheme. However, for us, there are only two choices when it comes to mixers – Kenwood or **KitchenAid** mixers.

The **KitchenAid** mixer has a metal construction, with fashionable retro styling. The darling of the modern cook, the company that makes **KitchenAid** mixers is located in St. Joseph, Michigan. The mixers come in a variety of bright, modern colors including scarlet, which is our favorite. The chrome version is the dream of the designer foodie, matching a whole host of desirable, "leave on the counter top" appliances. The advantage of a metal construction is that the mixer is quieter in operation, although neither brand should be thought of as silent! It is also more robust but, of course, these features carry a price tag, so you may need to consider what is right for you. The **KitchenAid** mixer has a range of optional attachments which cover the basic, time-consuming tasks that are tackled in the kitchen.

Kenwood offers The Chef and The Major, the latter being a large capacity machine suitable for domestic or light commercial usage. Both mix, whisk, and knead and have a wide range of attachments to take on many kitchen tasks, including a liquidizer for blending, making soups and drinks, and breadcrumbs. The original Kenwood Chef was all metal (apart from the bowl, which was glass). Now usually styled in white, with either a white or stainless steel bowl, Kenwoods are also available in colors, the choices having changed considerably over the years to match prevailing kitchen fashions. For fifty years or more, these machines have been made in the United Kingdom, and are now gracing the kitchens of busy cooks worldwide.

THE RIGHT TOOL FOR THE RIGHT JOB

This has always been, and still remains, a cooking teacher's favorite catch phrase! And it's quite right, too – you can't coax air into a mixture for perfectly light pastry or fluffy meringues and mousses, let alone knead bread dough for a perfect rise, with a blade in a food processor that has really been designed for chopping. Stand mixers have the following three basic blades, which are perfect for basic mixing jobs:

- The flat beater: the workhorse beater, to be used for cutting in butter or margarine, creaming, stirring meat and vegetable mixtures, and all general mixing and beating.
- The wire whip: for all whisking jobs, including egg whites, heavy cream, sponge and Angel food cakes, etc. Also great for beating the lumps out of sauces and custards!
- The dough hook: for kneading yeast mixtures into perfectly smooth, silky, and tensile doughs.

TO ATTACH THE BEATERS

With the mixer switched off, simply raise the head of your mixer and affix the required beater onto the mixer shaft, turning it slightly to lock into position. Unlock and remove the beaters in the same way.

The beaters are usually suitable for cleaning in a dishwasher, although we prefer to wash the metal beaters by hand to maintain their finish. It's great to be able to put the white coated blades of the **KitchenAid** mixer into the dish washer, and they do wash up very well, but remember to rinse them first, especially after making bread dough and if you are not going to run the dishwasher immediately.

Left Wire whip **Middle** Flat beater **Right** Dough hook

GETTING READY TO MIX

When you remove your mixer from the box, it should be perfectly adjusted and ready for use. A basic rule of thumb is that you should be able to just fit a sheet of paper between the beaters and the bottom of the bowl; use the flat beater to check. If adjustments should be necessary, it is simply done with the turn of a screw. Please refer to your mixer instruction book for details.

BASIC MIXING TIPS

As much common sense and a way to keep the kitchen free from flying flour as anything else!

• Always start mixing at a slow speed.

• Gradually add extra ingredients.

• Add ingredients down the side of the bowl or down the chute of the pouring shield to avoid excessive splashing while the mixer is running.

• Fold in fruit, flavorings, and flour at the end of recipes

using a very low speed to avoid knocking out the air.

• Some yeasted doughs that require blending or cutting the butter or margarine into the flour at the beginning of mixing are best started with the flat beater. However, it is important to change to the dough hook to mix in the liquid and to knead the dough.

• Whisking should always be started on a slow speed, and then gradually increased until the mixture is frothy, and then increased further to a faster whisking speed. Whisking too quickly will incorporate less air, leading to a closer-textured and heavier final result.

• Whisk egg whites at room temperature for the best possible results.

• Keep an eye on cream when whipping it. It can suddenly thicken, especially if you are whisking a large quantity. Adding a little milk and whisking again can sometimes rescue cream that has been whipped too much.

• We like to have two bowls for our mixers, which is

Left Rotor Slicer/Shredder   **Middle** Food Grinder   **Right** Pasta Maker

especially useful if you are making a mixture with egg whites added at the end, making bread and doing other cooking at the same time, or cooking for a party and making lots of different dishes.

ADDING ATTACHMENTS TO YOUR MIXER

We have selected our favorite table mixer attachments for this book, but you should check which of these are available for your mixer, and of course, check out other attachments designed for your machine.

ROTOR SLICER SHREDDER

One of the most useful attachments – and the one that you will see featured most frequently in our recipes. It is great for making salads and preparing bulk quantities of vegetables. There are two basic types of attachment, one

with drums and one with plates, the latter being "high speed," although both yield quicker results than a sharp knife even deftly wielded. Check out which type of attachment is available for your mixer.

We sometimes make potato casseroles for a quick dinner dish. Peel about two pounds of potatoes and process them through the Rotor Slicer/Shredder with two or three onions. Layer them in a buttered baking dish with lots of salt and pepper and about half a pound of marinated sardines or anchovies spread out between the layers and a sprinkle of sugar. Pour two cups of milk over the potatoes, drizzle the top layer with olive oil, and bake at 375°F for about an hour, until browned and the potatoes are tender. Serve with fresh green vegetables, or a green or a tomato salad. Coleslaw is also a favorite of ours, and it's so easy with this attachment. Slice half a cabbage into the mixer bowl, then grate in two carrots and one small onion using

Left Sausage Maker   **Middle** Citrus Juicer   **Right** Can Opener

the coarse shredder cone. Add plenty of salt and pepper and mayonnaise, then mix with the flat beater to combine.

FOOD GRINDER

This is another very useful attachment, good for making pâtés and essential if you wish to make your own sausages. It is also the best way of making homemade burgers, pasta sauces, and other dishes made with ground meat, because you can be utterly confident that you are using the best quality ground meat or poultry since you are grinding it yourself. The attachments come with two plates to offer a coarse or a fine grind. The best tips we can offer on usage are:

• Always be sure that the grinder shaft is properly located in the mixer power outlet, or the food will not be fed through the attachment.

• The knife goes onto the shaft before the grinder plate, and then the locking nut is used to hold the attachment together. Do not tighten it too much.

• Cut away as much gristle and sinew from the meat as possible (including "tubey" bits) as these tend to become tangled around the knife.

• Always cut meat into strips, not chunks, to feed through the grinder, and always use the stomper that has been provided to guide the meat through.

We sometimes use the grinder for preparing marmalade. It will not give quite as clear a result as cutting the peel by hand, but it does save a huge amount of time. Squeeze the juice from the fruit, pull out the membrane and pith, and tie it in a muslin bag as directed by your favorite recipe. Grind the peel using the coarse plate. Cooking time will also be shortened, as the peel will be in smaller and softer pieces than when cut by hand. We generally just boil the peel in the recommended amount of water until it has reduced as required – no additional simmering time appears necessary. Add the sugar and proceed as usual.

PASTA MAKER

We love making our own pasta, so a pasta making attachment is pretty important to us both. Some mixers have a pasta extruder, which will give macaroni-type shapes, but that requires a very dry dough being dropped into it in tiny pieces. Our favorite, though more limited in the shapes it can produce, is a roller-type attachment, which makes flat lasagne sheets as well as tagliatelle and linguine. After mixing the dough, it is passed repeatedly through the rollers until the sheets are smooth and of the required thickness, at which point cutting rollers can be fitted and the pasta cut into lengths.

- Always clear and lightly flour a large surface before making pasta so you have plenty of room to lay the lengths out without damaging them.
- Don't allow the dough to dry out at any stage in the process. If you have to leave the dough, always cover it with plastic wrap or a dish towel.
- Don't be afraid to roll the dough out over and over again. The more thorough you are during this part of the process, the better the end result will be. Under-worked dough will produce tough, chewy pasta.
- Depending on the quantity of dough, it is generally easier to divide it into manageable "lumps" (usually four) before feeding it through the rollers. This avoids getting tied up in long lengths of pasta, and makes it far easier to handle, especially when using the cutting rollers.

If you make your own pasta, and you certainly will with this attachment, it is a good idea to try to match the consistency of the sauce to be served with the shape of the pasta. Chunky sauces are best cooked with lasagnes, while smooth sauces are great with fine pastas, and those sauces with shrimp and small chunks are good with tagliatelle. Of course, these rules are not set in stone, but they do make eating pasta without getting splattered with sauce just a little bit easier!

SAUSAGE MAKER

Sausages are one of the largest and fastest growing sectors of the fresh meat market. Quick to cook and available in many designer flavors, they fit in well with hectic lifestyles and adventurous palettes. The sausage maker attachment is great fun and, again, it enables you to ensure that your family is eating the highest quality meat.

A certain amount of skill is required to produce a professional looking sausage, especially if you are going to twist them into links as they come through the attachment! You will need casing, which should be natural skins that your butcher can supply. (If you are unable to obtain these from your butcher, see page 158 for details of international distributors.) They have to be soaked and then threaded onto the attachment without splitting. Keep the skins in water until needed, and then catch a little water in one end to open it up for threading onto the attachment.

Grind your meat, and then mix it with seasonings and a small amount of breadcrumbs to bind it all together when mixed in the bowl using the flat beater. Try grinding a boned shoulder of lamb with a couple of shallots and one or two cloves of garlic, and then adding a small handful of pitted dates or dried apricots and grind them too, before passing some bread through the grinder to make breadcrumbs. Spice with mint, cumin, coriander, and a little crushed red pepper ground together. Remove the grinder plate and knife and fit the sausage stuffer, but ensure that the grinder drive shaft is still secure in the mixer power outlet. (Once you have meat all over your hands you won't want to be dismantling the attachment to see why the meat isn't coming through into the skins.) Feed the meat through slowly and evenly, holding the skins over the nozzle until they are sufficiently filled. Twist the skins every so often to form sausage links. We suggest that you leave the sausages for an hour or two before you cook them, which helps the meat to hold all its moisture.

CITRUS JUICER

For large quantities of juicing, this is a real time saver. Use it when preparing Grapefruit Sorbet (page 104), Seriously Lemony Lemon Bars (page 123), or any other recipe containing citrus. Of course, it's great for marmalade too, when used in conjunction with the grinder.

Left Grain Mill **Right** Fruit/Vegetable Strainer

Homemade lemonade is a real treat in the summer, especially after a hard game of tennis or even some serious relaxing! Pare the rinds of six large, unwaxed lemons with a potato peeler, place in a large pitcher with 1 cup superfine sugar, and add 8 cups of boiling water. Leave for one hour. Squeeze the juice from the lemons using the Citrus Juicer and add it to the pitcher, and then strain the mixture and chill, or serve over ice.

CAN OPENER

Keep your mixer out on the work surface with the can opener in place, and it will always be there, ready for action. This heavy-duty opener can tackle tiny cans of tomato paste all the way up to extra large cans of vegetables and coffee. Always keep the blades wiped clean and remove any paper and torn labels that collect and gather around the blades.

OTHER ATTACHMENTS

A strainer and a wheat or grain mill are among the other attachments available for stand mixers. The latter is useful for producing more unusual flours, either from beans or grains, especially for those who don't have access to health food stores.

Some attachments do the job of separate, stand-alone appliances, and it is up to you to decide which will get used the most – an attachment for your mixer to be fitted before use, or a counter top appliance. Always be sure that working parts of attachments and other appliances are suitable for cleaning in the dishwasher.

BLUEPRINTS FOR SUCCESS

Using your mixer is really very straightforward. Just select the appropriate beater and off you go. However, we have selected the tasks that our mixers are used for most frequently, and here are our hints and tips for culinary success.

If you have been used to creaming cakes with a wooden spoon and cutting butter into flour for pastry with your fingers, you will soon realize the meaning of the term 'labor-saving' appliance, as your mixer really does do all the hard work for you.

To get the very best results from your machine, however, it is important to know a little about the techniques and tasks that are being performed on your behalf – the basic science that supports cooking. Why should you use all-purpose flour with no raising agent for whisked sponges when you need flour and a raising agent for creamed mixtures? And why do we say self-rising flour plus additional raising agent when we make an all-in-one cake?

In this section we cover the culinary skills that you will tackle with your mixer, and we have explained the rules and basic theory behind each method. Of course, rules in cooking are there to be broken and many wonderful dishes are born through pushing the boundaries of flavor and texture combinations, but even the most exciting dishes are based on classical techniques. Exact proportions are critical for baking and puddings, as well as for pastries and mayonnaise, and these are the foundations of most of the dishes in this book.

We have also included some hints and tips as to how each mixture should be made – the best ingredients to use, the preferred method or order of mixing, any possible pitfalls to look out for, and occasionally, a rescue plan should anything go wrong! (Which it does for us all.)

Occasionally we say to use a beater that you might feel is an odd choice, but, rest assured, there is good reason for this! So, when we say mix the Lemonade Scones (page 131) with the dough hook on the slowest possible speed, we do mean the dough hook - although a classic scone would be mixed with the flat beater.

These blueprints will ensure repeated culinary triumphs for you and your mixer. Read them all now, or flick back and pick out the appropriate section before tackling a new recipe. Either way, it's all very useful information - and a vital ingredient for success.

SCONE DOUGH

A scone is a quick sweet or savory "bread" made without yeast. It is soft and light on the inside, and golden and crusty on the outside, served baked in a round or wedge-shape. Scones can be eaten warm or cold.

- Made from any variety of flours, either self-rising or all-purpose, and a leavening agent.
- Contains a small proportion of butter or margarine to flour.
- Butter or margarine can be used, although butter has a far superior flavor.
- Scones rise due to the chemical action of the leavening agent.
- Fresh milk, buttermilk, or yogurt is used to bind the mixture and to encourage the chemical leavening action.
- The texture should be light and fairly open.
- Scones are best eaten on day they are made.

BASIC METHOD

- Sift flour, leavening agent, and salt into mixer bowl.
- Add butter or margarine.
- Use the flat beater or dough hook at slow to medium speed to combine until mixture until it resembles breadcrumbs.
- Add nearly all the liquid, all at once.
- Mix again at slow to moderate speed until dough is smooth, springy, and elastic. Add remaining extra liquid if required.
- Roll out on a lightly floured surface to thickness of about ¾ inch.
- Cut into rounds or wedges.
- Put onto greased and floured cookie sheet.
- Brush with milk or beaten egg.
- Bake in preheated hot oven for about 10 to 15 minutes.

VARIATIONS

- Use wholewheat flour, or half wholewheat and half all-purpose flour.
- Add grated cheese or dried fruits.

BASIC HINTS FOR SUCCESS

- Handle the dough lightly.
- Keep the ingredients cool.
- Work quickly.
- Always preheat the oven.
- Always sift the flour before using, whether self-rising or all-purpose.
- Always sift the leavening agent, if using, with the flour so it is evenly distributed.
- Don't over work the dough, as this will result in heavy and badly risen scones.
- Don't over grease the cookie sheet, as this will encourage the scones to spread and loose their shape.

SHORT CRUST PASTRY

Short crust pastry is the most commonly used pastry as it is so versatile. It is also the easiest to make. Your mixer makes pastry quickly with a minimum amount of handling. It is made by the cutting in, or blending, method.

- Pastry of any description works because of accurately proportioned butter or margarine, flour, and liquid.
- Standard short crust pastry has a ratio of half butter or margarine to flour.
- Increasing the butter or margarine or type of fat will make the pastry even shorter.
- Butter, margarine, lard, or solid vegetable shortening can be used depending upon the desired flavor and texture.
- Butter alone produces a rich pastry.
- Butter and vegetable shortening makes a rich, light pastry.
- Adding egg yolk will make the pastry shorter, as the fat content is increased.

BASIC METHOD

- Sift the four and salt into the mixer bowl.
- Add the butter.
- Use the flat beater at slow to moderate speed until the mixture resembles breadcrumbs.
- Add ice-cold water a spoonful at a time until the mixture begins to come together.
- Use your hands to gather the mixture into a ball.
- Cover in plastic wrap and refrigerate for 30 minutes.

TO ROLL OUT

- Lightly flour a spacious surface.
- Use short, sharp movements away from you and work as quickly as possible, turning the pastry frequently to ensure that it does not stick to the surface.
- If rolling for a specific pan, allow for the base and sides of the pan, with a little extra to spare.

- The higher the butter or margarine content, the harder the pastry will be to roll out. Very short sweet pastry can be pressed into the pan with no adverse affect on the final result.
- Don't stretch your pastry or it will shrink during cooking. Also ensure that the pastry is pushed into the corners of the pan with your finger to keep a good shape.

TO COOK

- To bake pastry blind: line the uncooked pastry case with foil or wax paper and fill with pie weights, dried beans, or rice, and bake. Cool before filling.

BASIC HINTS FOR SUCCESS

- Always work quickly and with cold ingredients, utensils, and hands, and handle as little as possible.
- Do not over mix, as this will toughen the pastry.
- Too much liquid will also toughen the pastry.

SPONGE OR SANDWICH CAKES

These cakes are usually made by the creaming or whisking methods.

CREAMED SPONGE

- Creaming fat and sugar together incorporates air into the mixture. Insufficient creaming will result in a dense, heavy and/or coarse cake.
- Eggs are then added, a little at a time, and beaten well between each addition. Flour is folded in last, lightly at a slow speed, so as not to knock out all the air that has already been incorporated.
- The final mixture should be light and creamy.

BASIC METHOD

- Using the flat beater at moderate speed, "cream" the butter or margarine and sugar together until light, fluffy, and pale in color. Use superfine sugar or light brown sugar as their smaller crystals will incorporate into the butter or margarine better than other varieties with larger granules.
- Add beaten eggs gradually, combining fully after each addition.
- Add any liquid to the mixture and combine.
- Sift the flour, salt, baking powder (if using), and any additional ingredients into the mixer bowl in two or three stages at a slow speed. The final mixture is usually a soft, dropping consistency, and flicks easily off a spoon.
- Spoon into the prepared pan(s) and make a dip in the center to prevent the mixture from forming a peak during baking. This is particularly relevant if the mixture contains a high proportion of fruit.
- Bake in oven preheated to moderate to high heat.
- Usually position the pan(s) on the middle shelf.

BASIC HINTS FOR SUCCESS

- Measure and weigh ingredients as accurately as possible – correct proportions are essential.
- We strongly believe that where possible, butter should be used for making cakes. The flavor is undoubtedly superior.
- Use butter at room temperature or softened slightly.
- Use eggs at room temperature to prevent curdling. A curdled mixture will not hold as much air.
- If curdling occurs, add a tablespoon of flour and incorporate gently.
- Always sift flour and leavening agent.
- Always grease baking pans and base-line with wax paper unless otherwise stated.
- Always preheat the oven. Never open the door during cooking – the cake may sink.
- To test if cakes are cooked, press lightly – the mixture should be firm and spring back when touched.

VICTORIA SANDWICH

This classic cake is usually made using the creaming method above and is cooked in two pans of equal size. When cooked and cooled, the cakes are sandwiched together with jam and topped with a sprinkling of sugar.

Alternatively, fill with fruit, buttercream, whipped cream, fruit curd, sweetened cream cheese, or plain yogurt (see page 117).

ALL-IN-ONE METHOD

You can make an excellent sponge cake in very little time by beating all the ingredients together at once. This is particularly effective when using a mixer, as thorough beating is essential.

For success, however, the following guidelines apply:
- The butter or margarine must be soft to ensure that it incorporates easily.
- An extra leavening agent is required, as not engaging in an initial creaming process results in less air being incorporated into the mixture

BASIC METHOD

- Put all ingredients into the mixer bowl and combine using the flat beater at slow to medium speed. Use softened butter or margarine.
- Spoon mixture into prepared pan(s).
- Bake in a preheated oven.

WHISKED SPONGE CAKE

Your mixer is perfect for this method, as very thorough whisking makes a perfect cake. The sponge is made by whisking eggs and sugar together to incorporate air, and then adding flour to give it structure.

- All-purpose flour is always used for whisked sponges, as self-rising flour can cause the cake to rise too much and then collapse.
- No leavening agent is added.
- The texture is a light, open structure with a crisp surface.
- Due to rapid drying out, whisked sponges are always best eaten on the day they are baked.

BASIC METHOD

- Use the wire whip to whisk the eggs lightly, then add the sugar and whisk at full speed for about 10 minutes, or until the mixture leaves a trail when the whip is removed.
- The mixture will be pale in color and will have greatly increased in volume.
- Gradually fold in the sifted flour with a metal spoon.
- Pour into a prepared pan.
- Bake in a preheated oven.

BASIC HINTS FOR SUCCESS

Always use very fresh eggs at room temperature for better whisking.

- Use superfine sugar for a smoother, more even texture.
- Warm the bowl slightly before beginning the recipe.
- Use all ingredients at room temperature or slightly warmed.
- Always fold flour into the mixture gently with a metal spoon to avoid knocking out any air.
- Always preheat the oven.
- Usually position the pan(s) on a middle shelf.
- To test if the cake is cooked, press lightly and your finger should leave no impression in the cake.
- Remove from the pan and cool, right side up, on a wire rack to avoid getting patterns on the cake. Ensure that the cake does not cool in a draft, as a sudden change in temperature usually makes the cake shrivel.

MERINGUE

Made from egg whites (see note, page 4) and sugar, meringue can be dried out in the oven very slowly until crisp, or used as a soft topping when baked very quickly at a high temperature.

- The most common method of making a meringue is by adding dry sugar to whisked egg whites.
- Meringue may be piped, spread, or spooned into shapes.

BASIC METHOD

- Place egg whites in a scrupulously clean mixer bowl.
- Whisk the whites until very stiff and dry, starting slowly and getting faster.
- Add sugar a third at a time, whisking thoroughly between each addition. Alternatively, with the mixer and wire whip running at moderate speed, add the sugar a teaspoonful at a time, being careful not to over whisk.
- Spoon over a pudding, into pans, or pipe into required shapes.
- Cook very briefly in a very hot oven to serve as a topping.
- For dry meringue shells, cook at a very low temperature for a much longer period of time.

BASIC HINTS FOR SUCCESS

- Use eggs that are two to three days old, by which time the white will have lost some water through evaporation. This makes the whites more gelatinous and therefore easier to whip. The mixture is also easier to use in this condition.
- Traditionalists separate their eggs and let the white stand for 24 hours before using for the same reasons, although this is far from essential and rarely done in domestic kitchens today.
- Always use a spotlessly clean wire whip and bowl, as any

trace of fat or dirt will prevent the white from whisking satisfactorily.

- Always whisk in a cool environment.
- Use superfine sugar, as this is less damaging to the unstable proteins in the egg whites.
- Always add the sugar gradually and whisk it in thoroughly between each addition.
- Use the raw meringue immediately to prevent warm air from affecting the structure of the protein. If allowed to stand, the meringue will become watery and lose its shape.
- Never hurry drying meringue or you will produce soft, leathery results.
- Store dried meringues in airtight containers. They will keep for several weeks.

MAYONNAISE

Mayonnaise is a thick and creamy "emulsified" sauce where oil (traditionally olive) is dispersed and suspended in vinegar with the assistance of an emulsifying agent – egg yolk (see note, page 4). Mayonnaise is usually flavored with mustard, vinegar, lemon juice, salt, and pepper. It can be made effortlessly with the wire whip on your mixer.

BASIC METHOD

- Put egg yolks, mustard, salt, and pepper into the mixer bowl.
- Using the wire whip, combine at medium speed.
- With the mixer set at fast speed, add the oil very gradually, ensuring it is fully combined between each addition.
- The mixture will gradually thicken, increase in volume, and become creamy in consistency. The color will become whiter as beating continues.
- Add vinegar, lemon juice, and seasoning to taste.
- Refrigerate for up to two weeks before serving.
- If the mixture curdles, continue whisking and add a little vinegar or lemon juice. If this doesn't fix the problem, whisk more egg yolk(s) separately and gradually whisk the curdled mixture into it.

BASIC HINTS FOR SUCCESS

- Always use ingredients at room temperature.
- Always use the best quality oil you can afford.
- Never rush the addition of oil or the mixture will curdle immediately.
- Some people find an all olive oil mayonnaise too rich and strong in flavor, so experiment to find the right taste for you. Try light olive oil, or a mix of olive and grapeseed oils.

MOUSSE

A mousse is a light, whipped, sweet or savory mixture made easily with your mixer.

- It is usually made with a base of smooth fruit or vegetable purée.
- Stiffly whisked egg whites (see note, page 4) are often incorporated to open the texture of the mixture.
- Egg yolk can be added to create a richer mousse.
- Mousses are usually "set" with gelatin, cream, béchamel sauce, or sometimes mayonnaise.
- Generous seasoning is essential for savory dishes.
- Use quality ingredients to ensure a good flavor.

BASIC METHOD

- Use a clean wire whip to whip cream and other basic ingredients.
- Add dissolved gelatin and mix thoroughly; add a little of the whisked mixture to the dissolved gelatin and then whisk that into the mixture.
- Season very generously for savory dishes.
- Chill lightly. When starting to set, whisk egg whites and then fold them into the mixture.
- Pour into prepared molds and chill until set; aspic may be used as a base in the mold for savory mousses.
- Dip the molds in warm water to loosen and turn out.

BASIC HINTS FOR SUCCESS

- When dissolving gelatin, add it to hot water and stir. DO NOT boil gelatin.
- Use the correct ratio of gelatin to liquid.
- Always season mousse thoroughly, as chilling will inhibit most flavors.

BREAD

Bread is a baked dough usually risen by yeast. Using the dough hook on your mixer takes all the hard work out of bread making and saves on time, too.

- Most breads are made by combining flour with yeast and liquid.
- The dough is kneaded, left to rise, shaped, left to rise again, and baked.

- **The Flour** – the bulk of most bread dough. All-purpose flour, or bread flour, is preferable.
- All flour contains gluten, an elastic protein that is essential to hold the carbon dioxide that is given off by yeast. During and after baking, gluten hardens around the bubbles of carbon dioxide, thus giving the bread its risen shape.
- Kneading is required to stretch and strengthen the gluten, which makes it more elastic.
- The gluten becomes tough and leathery when baked if the dough is insufficiently kneaded.

- **The Yeast** – a natural leavening agent which gives off carbon dioxide as it grows.
- In order to grow, yeast must have moisture, warmth, food, and time.
- Sugar is essential if using regular dried yeast, as it "feeds" it. Fresh yeast will usually feed on the natural sugars in the flour. Honey can also be used.
- Salt is essential for flavor, but more importantly, it strengthens the gluten in the flour. This prevents the dough from rising too quickly.
- Butter, margarine, or oil is an important addition, as it adds moisture to the dough and improves keeping quality. It is not however essential.
- Milk, water, or a combination of the two may be used in the mixture. The amount varies according to the type of flour used.
- The temperature of the liquid should be just above body temperature. Too low a temperature won't activate the yeast, and too high a temperature will kill it.
- Fresh yeast – Usually found in a block, fresh yeast is similar in appearance to putty. It is fairly crumbly and can

be broken easily. If it is fresh enough, the yeast should have a fruity aroma. Stale yeast develops an unpleasant odor that will taint the bread. Fresh yeast is creamed with warm liquid to activate it.

- Dried yeast – Available in containers or individual packets, it is granular and light brown or beige in color. It must be rehydrated with warm liquid and activated with a small amount of sugar. It also needs about 15 minutes to "wake up" before use!
- Active dried yeast – Available in packets, this granular yeast is simply added directly to the flour together with remaining ingredients. Using active dry yeast usually means that the bread will only require one proving. Because manufacturers vary, always read the label.

BASIC METHOD

- Add the flour and salt into the mixer bowl.
- Cream the yeast with a little warm liquid. Alternatively, if using conventional dried yeast, add the packet and sugar to the warm liquid. The liquid should be just warm to the touch. (If using active dry yeast, add the packet to the flour, followed by the remaining ingredients.)
- Add to the flour and using the dough hook at slow to medium speed, combine the ingredients thoroughly.
- Knead for a few minutes until the dough is smooth and elastic and leaves the sides of the bowl.
- If using active dry yeast, shape as desired and leave to rise, covered, in chosen pan or on a cookie sheet for 30 to 40 minutes.
- For other yeasts, leave the dough in the mixer bowl, cover, and set aside in a warm place until the dough has doubled in size. Then, using the dough hook, knead again and shape. Leave in a warm place until doubled in size once more.

- Bake in a hot oven.
- To test for doneness, tap the bottom of the bread. It should sound hollow.

BASIC HINTS FOR SUCCESS

- Always use "healthy" yeast; check expiration date and ensure that the yeast smells and looks right before you begin.
- Always add salt for flavor, even if making sweet bread.
- Make sure the liquid to be added is at the correct temperature – it should be lukewarm, not hot.
- Always knead thoroughly to ensure even distribution of yeast and therefore gas.
- Unless using active dry yeast, never rush the kneading or proofing process.
- Let bread rise in warm conditions – too hot an environment will cause the dough to be heavy, too cool and nothing will happen.
- Always cook in a preheated hot oven.

LIGHT LUNCHES

Easy dishes for meals in a rush, these are favorite recipes for times when one course is just what you want, whether it's a substantial snack or a light main dish. Some of the recipes, such as our Creamy Corn Cornbread (page 32), require some preparation and a serious amount of cooking time, but then the finished dish is there as a substantial snack whenever you like.

GAZPACHO

SERVES 4 TO 6
PREPARATION TIME: 15 minutes
CHILLING TIME: at least 1 hour,
    preferably overnight

1½ lb ripe tomatoes, cores
    removed
1 red bell pepper, deseeded
1 green bell pepper, deseeded
1 red onion, peeled
½ cucumber, deseeded
2 garlic cloves, finely chopped
1 Tbsp finely chopped parsley
1 Tbsp finely chopped fresh
    basil leaves
1½ Tbsp red wine vinegar
½ cup crushed tomatoes
⅓ cup water
3 drops hot red pepper sauce
4 Tbsp olive oil
Salt and freshly ground black
    pepper to taste

Gazpacho is a classic summer soup from Spain and is easy to make with your mixer. This recipe does not use breadcrumbs — just fresh Mediterranean vegetables.

1 Coarsely grate the vegetables into the mixer bowl using the Rotor Slicer/ Shredder.

2 Add all the other ingredients and mix thoroughly with the flat beater, seasoning well with salt and pepper. Refrigerate for 12 hours if possible, to allow the flavors to mellow and blend (see Cook's Tip).

3 Serve this soup with cubes of frozen olive oil, some fresh basil leaves, and our Cheese Sablé crackers (see below).

COOK'S TIP: The gazpacho is best eaten chilled, when fresh, but it will keep well for up to 3 days in the refrigerator.

CHEESE SABLÉS

MAKES ABOUT 40
PREPARATION TIME: 15 minutes
COOKING TIME: 10 minutes

¼ lb cheddar cheese
¼ lb (1 stick) butter
1 cup all-purpose flour
Pinch of salt
Pinch of dry mustard

These lightest and richest of cheese crackers will disappear as quickly as you can make them! Great by themselves, or with Gazpacho.

1 Preheat the oven to 400°F and lightly butter two cookie sheets.

2 Grate the cheese into the mixing bowl. Add the butter, and cream together with the flat beater until light and soft. Add the flour, salt, and mustard and mix slowly until the mixture forms a stiff dough. Add just a little extra flour if necessary.

3 Roll the dough out on a lightly floured surface to ¼-inch thickness and cut into rounds approximately 1½-inches across. Arrange on the cookie sheets and prick lightly with a fork. Continue re-rolling the dough until it is all used up.

4 Bake for 10 minutes until lightly golden, then cool on a wire tray before serving.

SALMON AND CREAM CHEESE BAGEL PUFFS

Choux pastry, which is usually eaten filled with cream and topped with chocolate, is easy to make with your mixer. The pastry makes a great, light alternative to bagels for our favorite filling of smoked salmon and cream cheese – a perfect TV snack.

MAKES 6 PUFFS
PREPARATION TIME: 15 minutes
COOKING TIME: 45 minutes

⅔ **cup bread flour**
Pinch of salt
**2 oz (½ stick) butter, cut into
    small pieces**
⅔ **cup water**
2 eggs, beaten

FILLING
1 cup cream cheese
6 large slices smoked salmon
**Sliced gherkin pickles and
    capers**
**Fish roe, such as black herring
    or lumpfish (optional)**

**Lettuce, baby spinach leaves,
    or arugula and chives to
    garnish (optional)**

1 Preheat the oven to 425°F and lightly butter a cookie sheet. Sift the flour onto a paper towel and add the salt.

2 Melt the butter in the water in a saucepan over a low heat, then bring to a rapid boil. Add the flour and beat quickly with a wooden spoon until mixed, then pour into the mixer bowl and beat on a medium speed for one minute, or until the mixture leaves the sides of the bowl cleanly. Allow to cool for a few minutes.

3 Gradually add the beaten egg, mixing slowly at first, and then a little faster. The mixture should hold its shape, so only add as much of the egg as is necessary. Scoop the pastry out in six large spoonfuls and place on the cookie sheet, flattening the piles slightly into round, bagel-like shapes. Bake in the preheated oven for 25 to 30 minutes until browned and crisp.

4 Reduce the heat to 375°F. Carefully slit the puffs with a knife to allow the steam to escape and then bake for another 10 to 15 minutes until thoroughly dry and crisp. Cool on a wire rack.

5 To serve, split each puff with a knife and fill with cream cheese, smoked salmon, and gherkins or capers. Add the mock caviar and some salad leaves if you wish, then top with the remaining pastry and garnish with chives.

COOK'S TIP: Bread flour makes the crispest choux pastry.
It is essential to add the flour to the water and butter when it is boiling to get the correct consistency in the pastry; sifting the flour onto wax paper so that you can pour it straight into the saucepan is the easiest way to do this.

CREAMY CORN CORNBREAD

MAKES 1 LARGE LOAF
PREPARATION TIME: 40 minutes
COOKING TIME: 45 minutes

3 eggs, separated
14¾ oz can creamed sweet
   corn
⅔ cup heavy cream
¼ lb (1 stick) butter, melted
2 oz Gruyère cheese, finely
   grated
⅔ cup yellow cornmeal or
   instant polenta
1 cup self-rising flour
1 tsp baking powder
1 tsp superfine sugar
1 tbsp crushed red pepper
   (optional)
½ tsp salt

This loaf is almost a meal in itself – try it spread with cream cheese! It can also be sliced and served with cold meats or fish and salad. It's addictive!

1 Preheat the oven to 375°F and oil a 9-inch round cake pan with corn oil.

2 Beat the egg yolks with the corn, heavy cream, melted butter, and cheese on a low speed to combine, using the flat beater. Add all the dry ingredients and beat for a minute or so until completely blended. Transfer to another bowl and wash the mixer bowl.

3 Whisk the egg whites until stiff with the wire whip, starting slowly and gradually increasing to a medium-high speed. Fold the egg whites evenly into the corn mixture, then pour into the prepared cake pan.

4 Bake for 45 minutes until lightly browned and set. Loosen the cornbread from the sides of the pan and turn out carefully onto a wire rack. Cool slightly before slicing and serving.

COOK'S TIP: The cornbread will puff up slightly like a soufflé during baking, and then fall back a little – don't worry, this is normal!

LINGUINE WITH CHILE, CRAB, AND VERMOUTH

SERVES 4 AS A LIGHT MAIN COURSE OR APPETIZER

PREPARATION TIME: about 25 minutes

COOKING TIME: 5 TO 10 MINUTES

PASTA DOUGH:

2 cups all-purpose flour

2 eggs

1 egg yolk

FOR THE SAUCE:

2 oz (½ stick) butter

4 Tbsp olive oil

2 large cloves garlic, finely chopped

1 small red chile, finely chopped

12 cherry tomatoes, quartered

6-oz can white crab meat

2 Tbsp vermouth

3 Tbsp flat leaf parsley, finely chopped

Salt and freshly ground black pepper to taste

Lemon wedges to serve

Pasta is easy and quick to make with a stand mixer. Make it in advance, and when you're ready to eat, it takes less than two minutes to cook. Some people insist on using pasta flour, salt, and olive oil in their dough, but this recipe wins for us every time. We find regular flour ideal (and far less expensive!); salt can sometimes toughen the egg making the pasta leathery; and the addition of olive oil seems unnecessary.

1 Make the pasta. Combine the flour and eggs in the mixer bowl using the dough hook, initially at slow speed and gradually increasing to medium. Mix for about three minutes, then, if necessary, bring the dough together with your hands.

2 Cut the dough into four pieces and, using your pasta roller attachment on the lowest setting, run each piece of dough through the machine. Fold up the rolled dough and run it through again. Repeat this process about 10 to 15 times until the dough becomes shiny and almost leathery to the touch. Then, put the machine up a notch and feed the dough through again, continuing this process until you reach setting 5. Change the attachment to the linguine (fine) drum and feed each piece of dough through. Lightly toss flour through the pasta and reserve, well covered, in a cool place.

3 Bring a large pan of salted water to a boil. Meanwhile, heat the butter and oil in a large, deep skillet over a low to moderate heat. Add the garlic, chile, and tomatoes, turn the heat up to high, and cook for about 30 seconds. Add the crab, turn the heat up again if possible, and then add the vermouth and parsley. Cook quickly for about 30 seconds. Season generously with salt and pepper.

4 Add the pasta to the boiling water and cook for about 30 seconds. Drain thoroughly and transfer to the skillet, tossing well to mix.

5 Serve immediately with a mixed green salad and wedges of lemon.

COOK'S TIP: Always try to use organic, free-range eggs when making pasta, as the bright yellow yolks will produce a brightly colored yellow dough, which keeps its color even when allowed to dry before cooking.

POTTED CHEESE WITH GUINNESS

This appetizer or starter can be prepared in no time at all, and then chilled and forgotten in the fridge while you get on with other things! It features the wonderful combination of rich Guinness beer (a dark brown, stout-style beer) and sharp cheddar with an acidic creaminess that marries the flavors together.

....

1 Use the flat beater to cream the butter until really soft.

2 Attach the Rotor Slicer/Shredder and position the mixer bowl under it. Grate the cheese coarsely into the bowl, add all the remaining ingredients, and mix again with the flat beater.

3 Pack the mixture into a small bowl or ramekin and smooth the surface, then cover and refrigerate for at least two hours.

4 Remove from the refrigerator 20 minutes before serving to soften a little, and garnish with more freshly chopped parsley. Spread on Scallion Soda Bread (see page 37) or serve with crackers.

SERVES 4
PREPARATION TIME: 10 minutes
CHILLING TIME: 2 hours

3 oz (¾ stick) butter
2½ cups grated sharp cheddar cheese, preferably Irish
2 Tbsp sour cream
4 Tbsp Guinness® beer
4 drops hot red pepper sauce
2 Tbsp finely chopped parsley, plus extra for garnishing
Freshly ground black pepper to taste (you should not need salt – there's enough in the cheese)

EGGPLANT DIP

SERVES 6 TO 8
PREPARATION TIME: 10 minutes
COOKING TIME: 45 minutes,
   plus cooling time

2 medium eggplants
Lemon juice (see method)
About 1½ cups ricotta cheese
8 halves oil-packed sun-dried
   tomatoes, drained and
   finely chopped
1 clove garlic, crushed
12 green or black olives,
   pitted and roughly chopped
4 Tbsp finely grated fresh
   Parmesan cheese
2 to 3 Tbsp freshly chopped
   parsley
Salt and freshly ground black
   pepper to taste

This dish is fresh, flavorful, and creamy — ideal as a dip, a topping for bruschettas or tortillas, or served over a crisp salad. Add six to eight finely chopped anchovy fillets for a punchier flavor, if you wish.

1 Preheat the oven to 425°F. Prick the eggplants and bake for 40 minutes until the skins are blackened and wrinkled and the eggplants are soft. Cover with a wet dishtowel and leave to cool for 10 to 15 minutes. Peel the eggplants by pulling the skin off from the bottom end up to the stalk, and then quickly plunge them into cold water to which a squeeze of lemon juice has been added until completely cold.

2 Beat the ricotta in the mixer with the flat beater then add the eggplant cut into rough chunks. Beat on a low speed until smooth, then add the remaining ingredients and mix gently to combine. Season to taste, then scoop into a bowl to serve.

COOK'S TIP: Adding lemon juice to the water prevents the peeled eggplants from discoloring.

SCALLION SODA BREAD

A fabulously simple quick bread that is ideal with cheese or soup for an informal lunch or a light dinner.

SERVES 3 TO 4, MAKES 1 MEDIUM LOAF
PREPARATION TIME: 15 minutes
COOKING TIME: 20 to 25 minutes

1 Preheat the oven to 425°F and lightly butter a cookie sheet.

2 Blend the butter into the flours, salt, and baking soda using the flat beater. Add the chopped scallions and mix again.

3 Add the buttermilk and mix slowly, just long enough to form a dough; do not over mix or the bread will be heavy.

4 Knead lightly by hand on a floured surface, just enough to shape the dough into a round about 1½ inches thick. Any loose mix left in the bowl should be dumped out and incorporated at this stage. Place on the cookie sheet and with a sharp knife, score the bread, marking it into six pieces (do not cut all the way through).

5 Bake for 20 to 25 minutes until golden brown and set in the center. Cool on a wire rack and break or slice the bread into pieces before serving.

1 oz (¼ stick) butter
1 cup whole wheat flour
¾ cup all-purpose flour
½ tsp salt
½ tsp baking soda
3 scallions, trimmed and finely chopped
¾ cup buttermilk

SPICY GREEN PAPAYA AND VEGETABLE SALAD

SERVES 2

PREPARATION TIME: 30 minutes

1 medium green papaya, peeled and quartered, seeds removed

½ cucumber, cut in half lengthwise, seeds removed

2 carrots, peeled

2 Tbsp chopped unsalted and roasted peanuts

2 garlic cloves, finely chopped

3 to 5 green chiles, to taste

1 Tbsp sugar

1 ½ Tbsp lime juice

1 Tbsp Thai fish sauce

15 cooked shrimp (optional)

4 fine green beans, ends removed and broken into 1-in pieces

4 cherry tomatoes, halved

1 Tbsp finely chopped flat leaf parsley

3 mint leaves, finely chopped

This salad has the wonderful taste of Asia and is bursting with invigorating flavors and fragrances. You must use green, unripe papaya (the inside will be white) but, if you are unable to find this, leave the papaya out altogether and use cucumber (seeds removed) and carrot (peeled), or a mixture of both, instead. A ripe papaya will simply turn to mush used in this recipe!

1 First, grate the papaya and vegetables using the Rotor Slicer/Shredder fitted with the coarse shredding cone, then cover and set aside.

2 Prepare the dressing. Mix half the peanuts, garlic, and chiles in the bowl with the flat beater on the slowest speed for about three minutes, to really beat up the ingredients. Then, with the motor still running at slow speed, add the remaining ingredients, ending with the grated vegetables. Mix until thoroughly combined.

3 Serve on a large platter with the remaining peanuts sprinkled over the top of the salad.

VEGETABLE FRITTERS WITH FETA AND MIXED SALAD GREENS

This dish is ideal for lunch or as a light snack. Or, why not make mini fritters for parties or snacks?

1 Preheat the oven to 350°F. Coarsely grate the vegetables using the Rotor Slicer/Shredder. Catch them in a colander, and squeeze them hard with your hands to remove as much liquid as possible.

2 Whisk together the spices, cilantro, cornstarch, and egg in the mixer bowl, then season to taste with salt and pepper. Add the vegetables and mix well by hand, ensuring that all the vegetables are well coated in the batter.

3 Shape the mixture into eight round patties. Heat a small amount of oil (about ½ inch deep) in a large non-stick skillet over a moderate heat, and cook the fritters in batches until golden brown on both sides. You may have to add more oil during the cooking process. Transfer the fritters to a lightly oiled baking sheet and bake for 5 minutes.

4 Serve two fritters on each plate topped with a handful of greens and a sprinkling of crumbled feta.

COOK'S TIP: This dish is great with a really generous spoonful of caramelized onions – use 1½ lbs of onions and follow the method on page 72. Crumbled blue cheese is delicious in this dish if you are not a feta fan.

SERVES 4

PREPARATION TIME: 20 minutes

COOKING TIME: 20 minutes

1 medium zucchini, halved and seeds removed

1 medium sweet potato

1 medium onion

2 tsp ground coriander

2 tsp ground cumin

1 tsp paprika

4 Tbsp chopped fresh cilantro

¼ cup cornstarch

2 eggs, lightly beaten

Salt and freshly ground black pepper to taste

Oil for cooking

7 oz feta cheese, crumbled (if using a marinated cheese, drain it thoroughly)

Mixed salad leaves to serve

MID-WEEK
MEALS

In selecting our recipes for this chapter we have tried to keep preparation time to no more than about 30 minutes, a reasonable amount of time to spend in the kitchen while working and running a home too. Cooking times vary, but the family-style dishes are all contemporary and full of flavor.

SWEET POTATO AND ROASTED NUT LOAF

SERVES 4 TO 6

PREPARATION TIME: 20 minutes

COOKING TIME: 1 hour

⅓ cup cashew nuts, roughly
  chopped

⅓ cup pistachio nuts, roughly
  chopped

¼ cup sunflower seeds

¼ cup pumpkin seeds

1 large onion, diced

1 Tbsp olive oil

2 cloves garlic, finely chopped

2 tsp paprika

2 tsp cumin powder

1 tsp chili powder (optional)

2 eggs, beaten

2 Tbsp sour cream

1 medium (approx ½ lb) sweet
  potato, shredded using the
  coarse shredder cone

1 large apple, peeled, cored,
  and shredded using the
  coarse shredder cone

⅓ cup flat leaf parsley, finely
  chopped

1 cup fresh breadcrumbs

Salt and freshly ground black
  pepper to taste

The fact that this loaf is so tasty makes it being full of healthy ingredients an added bonus, rather than the main selling point! Serve with dressed salad greens or freshly cooked baby vegetables (smothered in butter if the healthy angle is not uppermost in your mind!)

1 Begin by roasting the nuts and seeds, keeping the pumpkin seeds separate from the others. This is a very important step and worth the effort, as their flavor will be hugely improved after roasting. Preheat the oven to 400°F. Spread the nuts and seeds out on a baking sheet and roast in the oven for about 10 minutes or until they start to become golden. Remove and allow to cool. Reduce the temperature of the oven to 375°F. Oil a 8½ x 4½ inch loaf pan.

2 Cook the onion in the olive oil over a low heat for about 10 minutes or until soft, then add the garlic and cook for another two minutes. Add the spices, salt and pepper, stir, cook for another minute, and then remove the pan from the heat.

3 Beat the eggs and sour cream together in the mixing bowl with the flat beater, then add the remaining ingredients, including all the nuts other than the pumpkin seeds, and combine on the slowest setting mixing briefly.

4 Spread the pumpkin seeds evenly over the bottom of the prepared pan, and then spoon the mixture in on top of them. Smooth the surface and bake for one hour.

5 Let the loaf cool in the pan for five minutes before turning out onto a serving platter and slicing. Serve hot or cold.

GARDEN PIZZA

SERVES 4 VERY GENEROUSLY
PREPARATION TIME: 40 minutes,
   including proofing time
COOKING TIME: 25 to 30 minutes

FOR THE PIZZA DOUGH:
4 cups all-purpose flour
1 tsp salt
1 Tbsp active dry yeast
1 Tbsp olive oil
1½ cups warm water

FOR THE TOPPING:
2 Tbsp olive oil, plus more for
   drizzling
1 large red onion, finely sliced
3 garlic cloves, finely chopped
½ lb baby spinach leaves
Salt and freshly ground black
   pepper to taste
8 baby asparagus, halved
   lengthwise
4 baby leeks, halved lengthwise
1 zucchini, cut into 2-inch
   spears
½ cup green peas (from frozen
   if necessary)
Ice water (see method)
2 oz mozzarella cheese, sliced
2 oz ricotta cheese
2 Tbsp freshly grated
   Parmesan cheese
4 Tbsp finely chopped flat leaf
   parsley
1 Tbsp finely chopped chives
12 black olives, pitted
Arugula, dressed with olive oil
   and lemon juice, for
   garnishing

This tasty pizza is a modern interpretation of an Italian classic and uses wonderfully young and tender baby vegetables for ultimate sweetness in flavor and crispness in texture. Your mixer makes light work of the dough.

1 First make the pizza dough. Combine the flour, salt, and yeast in the mixer bowl using the dough hook. Add the olive oil, then gradually add the warm water to make a soft, manageable dough. Continue kneading on a medium setting for about four minutes until the dough is smooth and elastic. Form into the desired shape (see Cook's tip below) and cover loosely with a damp cloth or plastic wrap. Leave the dough for about 40 minutes to rise.

2 Make the spinach topping while the dough is proofing. Heat the olive oil over low heat in a large saucepan. Add the onions and cook for five minutes, then add the garlic and cook for another five minutes, stirring frequently. Add the spinach and cover to allow the leaves to wilt, cooking about five more minutes. Season very generously with salt and pepper and allow to cool slightly. Blanch the remaining vegetables in boiling water for about one minute and then quickly immerse in a bowl of iced water, drain, and set aside.

3 Preheat the oven to 425°F. Drizzle olive oil over the risen pizza dough, spread with the spinach mixture, and top with the remaining ingredients, which should be evenly distributed over the whole pizza. Drizzle more olive oil over the topping and bake for 25 to 30 minutes, or until the dough and the cheeses are golden.

4 Serve sliced with arugula leaves dressed in olive oil and lemon juice piled high on top of each portion.

COOK'S TIP: We like to make one large rectangular pizza in a baking tray for ease of handling and cooking, but you can divide the dough in half and make circular pizzas with 12-inch diameters, if you prefer. The dough also freezes well if you don't wish to use it all at once.

CELERIAC, BACON, AND BLUE CHEESE GRATIN

This dish is ideal for mid-week meals as it is so versatile. Simply interchange these ingredients with those that you have available at the time. For example, almost any root vegetable can be used in place of celeriac, and other cooked meats, ham, and cheeses (such as strong cheddar, or nutty Gruyère) can also be substituted. Celeriac is also known as celery root.

....

1 Preheat the oven to 425°F.

2 Attach the Rotor Slicer/Shredder and using the coarse shredding cone, shred the bread to form crumbs and set aside. Then, using the shredding cone again, shred the celeriac into a large saucepan. Add the water to the pan, cover and "steam" for about five minutes. Meanwhile, cook the bacon in the sunflower oil so it just begins to crisp.

3 Drain excess liquid from the celeriac if there is any. Then, while it is still warm, add the butter, sour cream, mustard, thyme, and lots of salt and pepper, and mix well until the butter has melted.

4 Pour the celeriac mixture into a small casserole or gratin dish. Sprinkle the bacon and any remaining oil over the top for flavor, then dot with three-quarters of the cheese, followed by the breadcrumbs. Top with the remaining cheese. Bake for 15 minutes or until golden brown.

SERVES 4 TO 6
PREPARATION TIME: 25 minutes
COOKING TIME: 15 minutes

¼ lb stale (or minimum 1 day old) bread

1 large (approx 1¾ lb) celeriac, peeled and cut into manageable pieces

1 cup water

¼ lb (approx 6 slices) good quality bacon, cut into ½-inch pieces

1 Tbsp sunflower or vegetable oil

2 oz (½ stick) butter

½ cup sour cream

2 tsp dried mustard

1 tsp dried thyme

Salt and freshly ground black pepper to taste

¼ lb blue cheese (e.g. Stilton, Danish Blue), diced

ASIAN STYLE CRAB CAKES WITH MANGO AND AVOCADO SAMBAL

These crab cakes have a real taste of Asian flavor and are fantastic when topped with the accompanying sambal.

1 Prepare the sambal. Chop the mango and avocado into ¼-inch dice, then add the remaining ingredients and mix well. Set aside until needed.

2 Mix all the crab cake ingredients together except the egg white, cornstarch, sunflower oil, and sesame oil (if using) with the flat beater at a slow speed. Transfer to another bowl, wash the mixer bowl, and change the beater for the wire whip.

3 Whisk the egg white and cornstarch together on high speed until white and fluffy but not firm. Fold the egg whites gently into the crab mixture using a metal spoon, ensuring that it is well blended.

4 Form the mixture into four large, round patties, or into 16 miniature ones. Cook in about ½ inch of oil for about two minutes on each side (miniature cakes will take less time, about one minute) or until golden. Serve immediately with the mango and avocado sambal, and lime quarters.

SERVES 4
PREPARATION TIME: 15 minutes
COOKING TIME: 10 minutes

FOR THE MANGO AND AVOCADO SAMBAL:
½ ripe mango
1 ripe avocado
1 scallion, finely chopped
1 small birds eye chile, or Thai chile, seeds removed and finely chopped
1 Tsp Thai fish sauce
2 Tbsp lime juice
½ tsp sugar
1 Tbsp finely chopped fresh cilantro
½ Tbsp finely chopped fresh parsley

FOR THE CRAB CAKES:
1¾ cups white crab meat, well drained
2 scallions, including green tops, finely chopped
2 Tbsp finely chopped fresh cilantro
2 tsp lime juice
1 tsp light soy sauce
1 tsp Thai fish sauce
1 whole red birds eye chile, or Thai chile, finely chopped
1 stalk lemon grass, finely chopped
1 tsp fresh ginger, finely chopped
1 large egg white
1 tbsp cornstarch
Sunflower or vegetable oil for shallow frying
1 tbsp sesame oil (optional)

LAMB AND ROSEMARY CLAFOUTIS

SERVES 4

PREPARATION TIME: 15 minutes

COOKING TIME: 40 to 45 minutes

FOR THE BATTER:

1 cup all-purpose flour

¼ tsp salt

1 egg, beaten

1¼ cups milk

2 Tbsp roughly chopped fresh rosemary

4 lamb sirloin steaks, ¼ lb each

¼ cup all-purpose flour

Salt and freshly ground black pepper to taste

4 Tbsp sunflower or vegetable oil

This recipe is a twist on the traditional British Toad-in-the-hole, usually made from Yorkshire Pudding batter that puffs up around a sausage, and the French classic clafoutis which is traditionally made with cherries as a dessert. Our version is easy to make and serves four very heartily.

1 Preheat the oven to 425°F, and put a 1½-quart baking dish into the oven to heat up.

2 Make the batter. Combine all the batter ingredients in the mixer bowl, and using the wire whip, whisk quickly to remove any lumps and ensure a smooth mixture.

3 Cut each steak in half lengthwise. Then, put the flour, salt, and pepper into a large plastic resealable bag, add the meat, and shake until well coated. Heat the oil in a skillet and quickly fry the meat so it begins to color on each side. Pour the meat and oil into the hot baking dish, and working quickly, arrange the meat attractively, giving each piece its own space. Pour the batter over the meat and put it into the oven immediately.

4 Bake for 40 to 45 minutes or until the batter has risen and is golden in color. Serve immediately with green vegetables and onion gravy.

COOK'S TIP: To make onion gravy, simply fry three to four finely sliced onions in a little sunflower oil and butter, over a low heat, until caramelized and golden in color (about 10 minutes). Add a teaspoon of brown sugar, a splash of red wine and some gravy browning (according to manufacturer's instructions). Season to taste and whisk in 1 teaspoon of mustard, and 1 tablespoon of redcurrant jelly if liked. Bring to a boil, mixing continuously, then allow to cool slightly before serving.

TURKEY, HAM, AND EGG PIE

This is a real favorite with us, and a great way of using up leftover turkey after Thanksgiving or Christmas. However, now that cooked chicken is readily available in supermarkets and grocery stores, there's no excuse for this pie not to be a regular on the family menu.

1 Preheat the oven to 400°F and lightly butter a pie dish.

2 Make the sauce. Place the milk, flour, and butter in a pan and heat gently, stirring constantly, until combined and bubbling. Continue to cook for one minute and then season with salt and pepper to taste. Transfer to a bowl and allow to cool slightly.

3 Make the pastry. Blend the butter into the flour with the pinch of salt on a slow speed (using the flat beater) until the mixture resembles fine breadcrumbs. Add enough cold water to make a firm dough, then transfer to a lightly floured surface and knead lightly. Roll out to fit the prepared pie dish.

4 For the filling, mix the cooked meats, hard-cooked eggs, and capers into the sauce, then pour into the pie plate. Cover the filling with the pastry, crimping the edges and making a slit in the center of the crust to allow the steam to escape.

5 Bake the pie for 30 minutes until golden brown. Serve hot or cold.

SERVES 4
PREPARATION TIME: 30 minutes
COOKING TIME: 30 minutes

FOR THE SAUCE:
2 cups milk
4 Tbsp all-purpose flour
½ stick butter
Salt and freshly ground black pepper to taste

FOR THE PASTRY:
¼ lb (1 stick) butter
1½ cups all-purpose flour
Pinch of salt
Cold water (see method)

FOR THE FILLING:
7 oz cooked turkey, diced
7 oz cooked ham, diced
2 large hard-boiled eggs, peeled and chopped
2 to 3 Tbsp small capers

HOMEMADE BURGERS

SERVES 4 (MAKES 4 BURGERS)
PREPARATION TIME: 15 minutes
COOKING TIME: 4 to 8 minutes
   (rare to well-done)

1 lb good quality steak
½ tsp sea salt
½ tsp freshly ground black
   pepper (or green
   peppercorns, which are a
   great alternative)
1 small onion, finely grated
   (optional)
Oil for shallow frying if using a
   skillet

We prefer to use really good quality meat for our burgers and so add few extra ingredients to get the full flavor of the meat. The benefit of grinding the meat yourself is that you can choose the cut of meat and will know exactly how much fat is in the resulting mince. Select a good quality cut such as rump, sirloin, or top round.

1 Cut the meat into strips and then process using the food grinder. You can use either the fine or coarse grinding plate depending on personal taste, but we prefer the coarse plate for texture. However, if you are using a poorer cut of meat, you may find that the fine plate produces a more tender result.

2 Combine the meat with the other ingredients and mix well using the flat beater. Shape into four rounds, each about 1 inch thick.

3 Heat a large, nonstick skillet over medium heat, add the burgers, and cook for 2 minutes each side for rare meat, or 4 minutes per side for well done, turning once. Alternatively, grill or barbecue for 6 to 8 minutes, turning only once.

4 Serve the burgers as they are, or in buns topped with lettuce; a slice of Roquefort cheese; a little crispy bacon and avocado; fried mushrooms and Swiss cheese; or capers and sour cream.

VARIATIONS:

Grind best cuts of lamb and combine with:

- Chopped dried apricots and ground cumin and coriander

- Shredded parsnip and a little curry powder

- Chopped mint leaves and plain yogurt

Grind best cuts of pork and combine with:

- Shredded apple and sage

- Red currants and parsley

Grind chicken breast and combine with:

- Thai spices

- Grated lemon zest and thyme

- Chopped sun-dried tomatoes and basil leaves

COOK'S TIP: Shape the meat with wet hands to prevent the mixture from sticking to your hands.

TACO BAKE

This is Tex-Mex meets comfort food! Here, spicy ground beef is rolled in cheesy scone dough and baked, making a filling dinner for an active family. Serve with freshly cooked vegetables or a tomato and avocado salad.

SERVES 4 TO 6
PREPARATION TIME : 30 minutes
COOKING TIME : 25 to 30 minutes

I lb ground beef
Packet taco seasoning mix, or 2 Tbsp chili powder and I tsp ground cumin
I cup water
2 oz (½ stick) butter
2 cups self-rising flour
Pinch of salt
2½ oz cheddar cheese, grated
Milk to mix (see method)

I Brown the ground beef in a nonstick skillet, then stir in the seasoning or spices and cook for another minute. Add the water and simmer for 20 minutes.

2 Preheat the oven to 400°F. Blend the butter into the flour and salt in the mixer using the flat beater. Mix in most of the cheese, and then add the milk and mix on a slow speed to make a soft, manageable dough.

3 Turn the dough out onto a lightly floured surface and roll it into a rectangular shape the same length as a large loaf pan. Spoon the beef down the center of the dough. Working from the long side, roll the dough over the beef, encasing it inside the dough. Place in the lightly oiled loaf pan and scatter the remaining cheese over the top.

4 Bake for 30 minutes.

COOK'S TIP: For a creamy, cooling sauce to serve with the Bake, mix equal quantites of yogurt and sour cream, then add grated lemon rind and juice to taste, with chopped parsley, salt, and pepper.

QUICHE LORRAINE

SERVES 4

PREPARATION TIME: 25 minutes

COOKING TIME: 45 minutes

¼ lb (1 stick) butter, cut into
   cubes

1½ cups all-purpose flour

Pinch of salt

Cold water to mix (see
   method)

1 small onion, very finely
   chopped

4 slices good quality bacon,
   finely chopped

3 eggs, beaten

2 cups milk, or milk and light
   cream mixed

2½ oz Gruyère cheese, finely
   grated

Salt and freshly ground black
   pepper to taste

Nothing beats the mouthwatering taste of a well-baked quiche, with homemade pastry and a lightly set filling of cream and eggs with hints of cheese and bacon. Always use a metal pan to bake your quiche – china dishes will not allow the pastry to cook properly.

1 Place a cookie sheet in the oven and preheat to 425°F.

2 Prepare the pastry. Blend the butter into the flour and salt on a low speed using the flat beater until well blended. Add enough cold water to make a firm dough. Turn out onto a floured surface, knead lightly, roll out and use to line an 8 x 1½-inch pie plate.

3 Cook the onion and bacon together for five minutes over a gentle heat in a nonstick skillet. Spoon into the pie plate.

4 Beat the eggs into the milk and cream in a large bowl (using the mixer, or by hand), then add most of the cheese with some salt and pepper and beat again. Pour the mixture over the bacon and onion and scatter the remaining cheese on top.

5 Place the quiche on the hot cookie sheet and bake for 10 minutes. Lower the oven to 375°F and continue baking for another 30 to 35 minutes, until the filling is just set.

6 Allow to cool slightly before cutting. Serve the quiche warm or cold.

MEDITERRANEAN FISH PIE WITH CORNMEAL AND PARMESAN CRUST

A pie packed full of delicious seafood and topped with a crisp and unusual crust - this is a real favorite of ours.

....

1 First make the crust. Blend the butter into the cornmeal, flour, and Parmesan cheese using the flat beater until the mixture resembles breadcrumbs. Add the beaten egg and yolk and mix to form a soft dough. Cover and chill in the refrigerator until needed.

2 Preheat the oven to 425°F. Gently cook onion in the olive oil over a low heat for approximately five minutes. Add the garlic, eggplant, and pepper and cook for a minute or two longer. Stir in the paprika and parsley, and then turn up the heat and add the sherry. Stir continuously until the sherry virtually evaporates and then add the remaining ingredients (except the egg for glazing). Stir carefully, reduce the heat, and simmer for five minutes. Pour into a deep dish or pie plate about 9 x 1½ inches (about 1½-quart in volume).

3 Roll out the chilled cornmeal dough to fit the pie plate – it should be about ¼ inch thick. Use extra cornmeal to prevent it from sticking to the counter top. Decorate the edges of the crust with a knife or your fingers, then brush with beaten egg and sprinkle with extra grated Parmesan cheese. Bake for 10 to 15 minutes, until golden, then serve immediately.

....

COOK'S TIP: To economize, try using inexpensive fish fillets such as haddock, or ask your fish store attendant for a bag of mixed end cuts which often contain fabulous fish at a fraction of the price.

SERVES 4 TO 6
PREPARATION TIME: 25 minutes
COOKING TIME: 10 to 15 minutes

FOR THE CRUST:
¼ lb (1 stick) butter, cut into small pieces
½ cup cornmeal
⅓ cup all-purpose flour
⅓ cup finely grated Parmesan cheese, plus extra to finish
1 egg, beaten
1 egg yolk

FOR THE FILLING:
1 Tbsp olive oil
1 large red onion, roughly chopped
2 large cloves garlic, finely sliced
1 medium eggplant, cut into ½-inch dice
1 large red bell pepper, cut into ½-inch dice
½ tsp paprika
2 large handfuls flat leaf parsley, chopped
2 Tbsp dry sherry
14½-oz can diced tomatoes
½ cup water
½ tsp salt
2 tsp raw sugar
Few drops hot red pepper sauce (optional)
½ lb fresh mixed prepared shellfish (e.g. mussels, shrimp, calamari, clams)
½ lb thick cod fillets, skinned and diced in chunks
1 egg for glazing

CREAMY FISH BAKE

SERVES 4
PREPARATION TIME: 15 minutes
COOKING TIME: 45 minutes

1 cup cream cheese
1 cup sour cream
⅔ cup milk
3 eggs
1 to 2 Tbsp horseradish,
   or 1 tsp wasabi
Salt and freshly ground black
   pepper to taste
About 1 lb smoked mackerel
   or smoked trout
6 to 8 scallions, trimmed and
   sliced
6 to 8 slices ciabatta
Paprika for garnishing

Mix this up in next to no time, and then take the time to relax while this delicious fish bake is in the oven. We like using smoked mackerel or smoked trout, but you could try smoked haddock or cod as an alternative.

1 Preheat the oven to 375°F and lightly butter a large gratin dish.

2 Beat the cream cheese and sour cream until smooth in the mixer using the flat beater, then add the milk, eggs, horseradish, and salt and pepper and beat again.

3 Skin the mackerel and break into large flakes, then add it to the bowl along with the scallions and mix to combine on a slow speed.

4 Line the sides of the dish with ½-inch slices of the bread, then pour in the mackerel cream. Sprinkle a little paprika over the top and bake for 45 minutes, or until set. Serve immediately.

CARROT AND CILANTRO SOUFFLÉ

SERVES 3
PREPARATION TIME: 20 minutes
COOKING TIME: 40 to 45
   minutes

2 oz (½ stick) butter
2 heaping Tbsp all-purpose
   flour
1 Tbsp ground coriander
½ tsp ground turmeric
1 cup milk
6 eggs, separated
2 to 3 carrots, finely grated
2 Tbsp chopped cilantro
Salt and freshly ground black
   pepper to taste

Don't let the thought of making a soufflé be a worry — just think of it as white sauce with egg whites folded in! Quick to make, light, and very tasty, this is a perfect mid-week munch, especially if you are tired and eating late, and don't want anything too heavy.

1 Preheat the oven to 350°F. Lightly butter an 8-inch soufflé dish (about 6 cups capacity).

2 Melt the butter in a large pan, add the flour and spices, and beat well. Cook over low heat for one minute or so, then gradually add the milk, beating well after each addition. The mixture will be very thick. Cook for another minute, stirring constantly, and then cool slightly.

3 Add the egg yolks and beat thoroughly, then stir in the grated carrots, cilantro, and salt and pepper to taste.

4 Meanwhile, whisk the egg whites in the mixer until very stiff , starting slowly and then increasing the speed. Fold the whipped egg whites into the carrot mixture, a little at a time, using a metal spoon. Scrape the mixture into the prepared dish and bake for 40 to 45 minutes until set. Serve immediately.

CHORIZO AND MOZZARELLA STUFFED MUSHROOMS

These mushrooms are ideal for a mid-week meal, as they are incredibly quick and easy to make. They use ingredients that are very easy to come by, or that you might well have in the refrigerator or pantry.

1 Preheat the oven to 400°F. Grease a cookie sheet.

2 Wipe each mushroom clean with a damp cloth and carefully remove the stems, setting them aside. Place each mushroom on the prepared cookie sheet, stem-side up. Divide the spinach equally among the mushrooms, making sure that no spinach sticks out over the edges.

3 Shred the mushroom stalks, bread, garlic, mozzarella cheese, and chorizo into the mixer bowl using the fine shredding cone on the Rotor Slicer/Shredder. Add the thyme, crushed red pepper (if using), and a generous amount of salt and pepper, and mix thoroughly with the flat beater. Pile the mixture onto the mushrooms and press down gently with the palm of your hand. Drizzle with olive oil, and scatter Parmesan cheese over and bake for 10 to 15 minutes. Serve with a large salad and new potatoes or warmed crusty bread.

COOK'S TIP: Instead of chorizo and mozzarella, use other cooked meats or hams (preferably with a strong flavor) and any cheese that melts well. Arugula or other young greens can be used in place of spinach and the herbs can be varied, too.

SERVES 4

PREPARATION TIME: 10 to 15 minutes

COOKING TIME: 10 to 15 minutes

4 large portabello mushrooms

Small handful baby spinach leaves

3½ oz (about 4 slices) stale bread, minimum 1 day old

1 clove garlic, peeled

About ⅓ lb mozzarella cheese

2 oz smoked chorizo sausage

1 Tbsp fresh thyme

Pinch crushed red pepper (optional)

Salt and freshly ground black pepper to taste

2 Tbsp olive oil

Grated Parmesan cheese to sprinkle over the top

EASY ENTERTAINING

Is there such a thing? Well, with a stand mixer to do the major mixing jobs for you, there certainly is! Guests are always bowled over by homemade food, and our selection of dishes yields fabulous results without too much effort. There's a mixture of chef-inspired, stylish dishes that are straightforward when following our directions, as well as some more relaxed dishes for informal, "kitchen table" dinners.

LOBSTER RAVIOLI WITH SPARKLING ROSÉ AND PINK PEPPERCORN SAUCE

SERVES 4

PREPARATION TIME: 2 hours and 20 minutes

COOKING TIME: 1 to 2 minutes

FOR THE STOCK:

2 shallots, diced

1 carrot, diced

1 celery stalk, diced

1 leek, diced

1 bouquet garni (tie some thyme, parsley, and a bay leaf to half a celery stick with string)

Juice of half a lemon

4 cups water

Shell from 1 lobster

FOR THE FILLING:

Tail and claw meat from 1 small cooked lobster (about 1 lb), shell reserved for stock

½ cup heavy cream

1 egg, beaten

Pinch of cayenne pepper

Salt and freshly ground black pepper to taste

This dish is very special and well worth the effort. Don't be put off by the seemingly complicated nature of the recipe or the time involved in making it. Each step is actually very easy to follow, and much of the time is simply due to slow cooking or cooling as opposed to hard work! The final dish need not be expensive either, because despite the initial outlay for the lobster, making the pasta and sauce yourself makes this an economical option for entertaining.

1 Begin by making the stock. Put all the ingredients into a large pan and bring to a boil, then reduce the heat and simmer for one hour. It will have reduced by one quarter. Allow to cool completely, with the shell still in the stock.

2 Meanwhile, make the lobster filling. Finely chop the lobster meat. Using the wire whip, whip the cream until thick, add the egg and seasoning, and whisk again before adding the lobster and combining carefully. Refrigerate until needed.

3 Begin the sauce by melting half the butter in a large saucepan, and then adding the shallots. Cook for about 10 minutes over low heat, or until the shallots are translucent and soft. Add the rosé and reduce until the pan is almost dry. Turn off the heat and leave until needed.

4 When the stock is cool, drain it through a large sieve or colander, reserving the liquid and discarding the shells and vegetables. Add the stock to the sauce and bring it back to a boil before lowering the heat slightly and reducing by approximately two-thirds of its original volume. This will take about 20 to 30 minutes.

5 While the sauce is reducing, make the pasta dough. Use the dough hook to combine the ingredients until they come together. Fit the pasta maker and run the dough through the standard roller on the lowest setting at least 15 times, folding the dough back on itself between each rolling. Divide the dough into four and begin rolling each piece at setting 2, repeating the process at each

ascending setting until you reach setting 5. Lay the four pieces of dough out on a well-floured surface and cut into 3-inch wide strips with a sharp knife. You should have 20 rectangular strips.

6 Remove the lobster filling from the refrigerator. Put about 1 teaspoon of filling about 1 inch from the bottom end of each pasta strip. Use your finger to smooth a little water around each mound of filling, and then fold the top of the strip down over it. Press down around the filling and seal firmly. Place each ravioli on a floured tray, cover, and refrigerate while you finish the sauce.

7 When the sauce has been reduced, add the sour cream, tomato paste and seasonings (except the basil leaves) and whisk in the remaining butter until melted and combined. Remove from the heat until needed.

8 When you are ready to eat, bring a large pan of salted water to a boil and heat the sauce gently. Drop the ravioli into the water and cook for about one to two minutes. Serve five ravioli per person on warmed plates and pour the hot sauce over the top. Scatter with the shredded basil and serve immediately.

FOR THE SAUCE:
2 oz (½ stick) butter, divided
2 shallots, finely chopped
1 cup sparkling rosé (blush)
brut
Fish stock (see above)
3 Tbsp sour cream
1 Tbsp tomato paste
1 tsp pink peppercorns
Pinch of cayenne pepper
Salt to taste
10 basil leaves, finely shredded

FOR THE PASTA DOUGH:
2 cups all-purpose flour
2 eggs
1 egg yolk

INDIVIDUAL WILD MUSHROOM AND THYME TARTS

Individual tarts look very attractive and professional and take only a small amount of extra effort. These tartlets are a fabulous appetizer, or equally wonderful as a light main course served with a large mixed green salad.

1 Make the pastry. Sift the flour, salt, and thyme together in the mixer bowl. Add the butter and mix using the flat beater at slow speed until the contents resemble breadcrumbs. Beat in the yolk and then the water, adding a tablespoon at a time (you may not need it all) until the mixture comes together as a dough. Wrap in aluminum foil or plastic wrap and refrigerate for 30 minutes.

2 Meanwhile, preheat the oven to 400°F. Grease six individual tart pans that have removable bottoms (4¼ x 1¼ in).

3 Roll the pastry out on a floured surface to about ¼-inch thickness. Using a 5½-inch round cookie or biscuit cutter, cut out six circles and line each tart pan with the pastry, pushing the dough down firmly into the edges of the pans. Remove any surplus pastry by passing a rolling pin over the top of each pan; this will also give you a professional finish. Prick the bases thoroughly with a fork, and bake for 15 minutes or until lightly golden. Remove from the oven and reduce the temperature to 325°F.

4 Meanwhile, make the filling. Melt the butter in a medium skillet over medium heat. Add the mushrooms and sauté briefly before adding the garlic and stirring thoroughly. Allow the mushrooms to get a little brown as they cook, turning up the heat if necessary. Add the sherry and cook over a high heat until it has virtually evaporated, then add the thyme and stir well. Allow to cool slightly before dividing the mixture evenly between the tarts.

5 Beat together the eggs, sour cream, and Parmesan cheese and pour the mixture into each tart, leaving about a ¼ inch of pastry showing at the top. Sprinkle with a little extra Parmesan cheese and bake for 30 to 40 minutes or until golden and set. Serve the tarts warm, or cold, piled with arugula leaves dressed with balsamic vinegar.

SERVES 6
PREPARATION TIME: 30 minutes
COOKING TIME: 45 to 55 minutes

FOR THE PASTRY:
1 cup all-purpose flour
Pinch of salt
1 tsp dried thyme
½ stick butter, chilled and diced
1 large egg yolk
2 Tbsp cold water

FOR THE FILLING:
1 oz (¼ stick) butter
½ lb mixed store-bought wild mushrooms, roughly chopped
2 cloves garlic, finely chopped
1 Tbsp dry sherry
1 tsp dried thyme
2 eggs, beaten
½ cup sour cream
2 oz fresh Parmesan cheese, finely grated, plus more for garnishing

STEAK, MUSHROOM, AND OYSTER PIE

SERVES 4 TO 6

PREPARATION TIME: 2 hours 35 minutes, including chilling time for the pastry

COOKING TIME: 1½ to 2 hours

FOR THE ROUGH PUFF PASTRY:

2 cups all-purpose flour

¼ tsp salt

7 oz (1¾ sticks) butter

1 tsp lemon juice

About 4 Tbsp ice-cold water

FOR THE FILLING:

1 lb boneless chuck or blade steak, trimmed and cut into ¾-inch cubes

3 Tbsp seasoned flour (all-purpose flour mixed with salt, pepper and 2 tsp mixed herbs)

2 medium onions, chopped

3 oz whole baby button mushrooms, cleaned

12 oysters, freshly shucked with liquor reserved, or canned

1 Tbsp oyster sauce

4 Tbsp red wine

½ cup reduced beef stock

1 beaten egg or milk for glazing

This British classic is just as tasty as it has always been. The method may seem very long-winded, but much of the time is spent chilling the pastry or slow cooking the pie, so you can concentrate on preparing for your guests. Of course, if you have the pastry prepared already there is very little to be done. To make the reduced beef stock, simmer 1 cup stock over a medium heat until half its original volume.

1 Make the pastry. Sift the flour and salt into the mixer bowl, and add the butter. Using the flat beater at a slow speed, roughly combine the ingredients; the butter should remain in lumps. Add the lemon juice and enough ice-cold water, a spoonful at a time, to make a soft, but very lumpy dough. Draw into a ball with your hands and place on a lightly floured surface.

2 Roll the dough out into a rectangular shape (about 10 x 6 inches). Then, fold the top third of the pastry over the middle third of the rectangle, and the bottom third over that. Give the dough a 90-degree turn and roll out again to make the same size rectangle. Repeat the folding process. Cover in plastic wrap and chill in the refrigerator for 30 minutes, then repeat rolling and folding as above. Do this — rolling, folding, and chilling — four times in total, by which time the dough should be smooth. Cover and chill again until required.

3 Prepare the filling. In a plastic resealable bag, toss the steak in the seasoned flour until evenly covered. Transfer the meat to an 8 x 1½-inch pie plate and add the onion, mushrooms, and oysters. Mix well with your hands to ensure an even distribution of ingredients. If using fresh oysters, include the liquor at this time and exclude the oyster sauce. In a small bowl, mix the oyster sauce (if using), red wine, and reduced stock together before pouring over the meat in the pie plate.

4 Preheat the oven to 450°F. Roll the pastry out on a floured surface to about a ¼-inch thickness. Cut a strip from the outside edge of the pastry. Moisten the edge of the pie dish with a little water and stick this strip to it. Trim off any excess. Moisten this strip before placing the rolled pastry over the pie dish. Seal and trim the edges before decorating, either by pinching them with thumb and forefinger, or by making indentations by pressing into them with the prongs and forefinger, or by making indentations by pressing into them with the prongs of a fork. Make a small hole in the top of the pie to allow the steam to escape and decorate with the remaining pastry, if you wish. Brush with a little beaten egg or milk to glaze.

5 Bake the pie for 10 minutes or until the pastry has risen and is golden brown, then cover the pie with a loose "tent" of aluminum foil and lower the temperature to 350°F. Cook for another 1½ to 2 hours, or until the meat is tender when tested through the crust with a skewer. Serve immediately with fresh vegetables and creamy mashed potatoes.

SERVES 4 TO 6

PREPARATION TIME: 2 hours
and 25 minutes, including
chilling time for the pastry

COOKING TIME: 30 to 35
minutes

FOR THE CURRY PASTE:

1 large stalk lemon grass,
finely chopped

2 Tbsp peeled and finely
chopped gingerroot

½ tsp finely chopped lime zest

4 small green chiles, finely
chopped (with seeds if you
like your curry hot)

3 garlic cloves, finely chopped

2 shallots, finely chopped

¼ tsp coriander seeds

¼ tsp cumin seeds

¼ tsp salt

¼ tsp ground turmeric

FOR THE ROUGH PUFF PASTRY:

2 cups all-purpose flour

¼ tsp salt

1¾ sticks butter

1 tsp lemon juice

Milk or beaten egg to glaze

FOR THE CURRY FILLING:

1½ cups coconut milk

2 large boneless chicken
breasts, thinly sliced

½ tbsp sugar

1 tbsp Thai fish sauce

¼ lb eggplant, cut into ½-inch
cubes

¼ lb green beans, cut into
1-inch lengths

3 kaffir lime leaves, torn into
pieces with stems discarded

10 Thai basil leaves

THAI CHICKEN PIE

East meets West! This pie combines a family favorite with exciting Asian flavors.

....

1 Make the pastry following the method on page 68 (Steak, Mushroom, and Oyster Pie). Cover in plastic wrap and set aside in the refrigerator to chill for two hours.

2 Make the curry paste. Put all the ingredients except the turmeric into the mixer bowl, and using the flat beater, mix the ingredients at medium speed for about 10 minutes or until a rough paste is achieved. You may need to stop the machine intermittently to push the contents back into the bottom of the bowl. Then, using a metal spoon, stir in the turmeric and set aside.

3 Next, make the filling. Put two spoonfuls of coconut milk into a wok or large saucepan. Stir gently on a low heat until the coconut oil begins to separate from the milk; this will be very obvious when it happens. Add the curry paste and stir until there is a distinct smell of chiles (the best test is to sniff the contents of the pan, and if it makes you sneeze, then it's ready!) Add a little more coconut milk if the pan has become too dry, and then add the chicken, sugar, and fish sauce. Stir until the chicken turns white, then pour in the rest of the coconut milk. Turn up the heat a little and add the eggplant and beans. Cook on a high heat for about five minutes to reduce the mixture, and then remove from the heat. Add the lime leaves and basil.

4 Preheat the oven to 400°F. Divide the pastry in half and roll out into two rectangles (about 12 x 8 inches). Lay one piece on a lightly floured cookie sheet and spoon the chicken mixture over it, leaving about an inch border on all sides. Brush a little water around the edges and lay the second rectangle of pastry over the top, squeezing the edges together and being sure to thoroughly seal the pastry so there is no chance of the filling escaping. Use your thumb and forefinger to flute the edge and make it look more attractive. Brush with milk or beaten egg to glaze, and cut two or three little holes in the top to let the steam out.

5 Bake the pie for about 30 to 35 minutes, or until it has puffed up and is a rich golden color. Eat hot, or allow to cool.

ROASTED ONION TART WITH BALSAMIC VINEGAR

SERVES 6

PREPARATION TIME: 40
  minutes

COOKING TIME: 30 minutes

FOR THE FILLING:

1½ lb onions

6 whole cloves garlic, peeled

3 bay leaves

6 sprigs fresh thyme

Salt and freshly ground black
  pepper to taste

3 Tbsp olive oil

1 Tbsp balsamic vinegar

FOR THE BASE:

3 Tbsp sesame seeds

1½ cups all-purpose flour

½ tsp salt

1 egg, beaten

3 Tbsp olive oil

Water to mix

Slow-cooked onions make a deliciously rich vegetable filling for numerous tarts and pies, and this is one of our favorite recipes. As an alternative to roasting, simmer the onions slowly for an hour or more. The filling can also be used by itself as an onion relish (see page 41). Use the best balsamic vinegar you can afford.

1 Preheat the oven to 425°F. To make the filling, slice the onions into a large roasting pan using the Rotor Slicer/Shredder, and add the garlic, bay leaves, and thyme. Season well with salt and pepper, drizzle with the olive oil and balsamic vinegar, and toss to mix. Roast for 30 minutes, stirring once.

2 Meanwhile, prepare the base. Mix the sesame seeds with the flour and salt in the mixer bowl using the flat beater, then add the egg, oil, and as little water as is necessary to make a firm dough. Lightly flour a cookie sheet and roll the base out on it to make about a 10-inch circle.

3 Season the onions again; they should be soft but not too brown. Scoop them onto the base, removing the herbs. Drizzle with a little more olive oil and balsamic vinegar and bake for 30 minutes.

FILLED SAVORY BRIOCHE

MAKES 12 BRIOCHE, SERVES 6
PREPARATION TIME: about 1½ hours, including rising time
COOKING TIME: 15 minutes

FOR THE BRIOCHE:
2 cups all-purpose flour
1 Tbsp active dry yeast
3 Tbsp milk
¼ lb (1 stick) butter, melted
1 tsp superfine sugar
½ tsp salt
2 eggs, beaten

FOR THE FILLING:
1 Tbsp olive oil
1 red onion, halved and sliced
1 clove garlic, finely chopped
2 giant handfuls (about ½ lb) baby spinach leaves
2 oz feta cheese, cubed
12 oil-packed sun-dried tomatoes, drained
12 small marinated hot peppers
12 pitted black olives

1 beaten egg or milk to glaze

These savory brioche are perfect for entertaining at buffets, parties, or picnics. They can be made with any filling you choose, and because they freeze well, they can be made in advance — although they are undoubtedly best eaten on the day they are baked. Keep the filling on the dry side and don't be tempted to be overly generous or it will just ooze out during cooking.

1 Make the brioche. Put all the ingredients into the mixer bowl and mix well with the dough hook for 2 to 3 minutes at a moderate speed. The dough will be rather sticky, but don't worry. Bring it together with your hands and allow it to rise in the mixer bowl covered with plastic film, in a warm place for 1 hour.

2 Meanwhile, make the filling. Heat the olive oil in a large pan and add the onion. Cook slowly for about eight minutes, then add the garlic and cook for another two minutes. Stir in the spinach, turn off the heat, cover, and leave for about five minutes, or until the spinach is wilted. Set aside and allow to cool until needed.

3 Punch down the dough using the dough hook, and knead again for about three minutes. Divide the dough into 12 balls, and roll each one into a 4-inch circle. Put a tablespoon of the spinach into the center of each, then add a cube of feta and one each of the sun-dried tomatoes, hot peppers, and olives.

4 Moisten the edges of the dough with water or milk, and gather the dough around the filling to form a ball. Place with the seams down on a cookie sheet and let rise for about 15 minutes. Preheat the oven to 450°F.

5 Brush the tops with the egg or milk to glaze, and bake for about 15 minutes until golden. Serve warm, or allow to cool completely and eat cold. Cool slightly before serving warm, as the filling will be very hot.

BAKED SPICED PORK TERRINE

A homemade terrine is a glorious appetizer – full of top quality meat, and spiced in a more adventurous way than a store bought pâté. Make two while you are in the mood and freeze one for later. It will keep for up to three months in great condition. Ask your butcher to provide you with pig's liver – if this is not available, chicken liver is a good alternative.

....

1 Preheat the oven to 350°F. Line the base of two large loaf pans with wax paper.

2 Stretch the bacon slices gently with the back of a knife, making them thinner as you pull. Use the stretched pieces to line the prepared pans, leaving the ends of the bacon dangling over the sides for now.

3 If necessary, remove the skin from the pork and cut the meat into long strips. Trim the liver and cut that into pieces of a similar size.

4 Heat a small skillet until hot, then add the fennel seeds and dry roast them for 30 seconds or so, until fragrant. Transfer to a mortar and pestle and grind, or crush them with the end of a rolling pin on a cutting board. Place the sausage in the mixer bowl, break it up slightly with the flat beater, and add the crushed fennel.

5 Set the food grinder fitted with the coarse plate onto the mixer. Grind the pork, liver, and garlic into the bowl of sausage, pressing the meat through with the stomper supplied. Add the crushed red pepper, salt, and pepper, and mix well with the flat beater. Divide the mixture between the prepared pans, pressing it down evenly, then fold the bacon over the meat and cover the pans with aluminum foil.

6 Place the terrines in a small roasting pan, then fill the roasting pan with boiling water until it comes halfway up the sides of the terrines. Bake in the water bath in the oven for two hours, then allow to cool completely.

7 Press the terrines in the pans by placing heavy weights or pans filled with cans on the aluminum foil covering. Refrigerate with the weights overnight.

8 Loosen the terrines with a thin knife, then turn them out, scraping away any jelly and juices. Serve sliced with hot toast, gherkin pickles, mustard, or chutney.

MAKES 2, EACH SERVES 6 TO 8
PREPARATION TIME: 30 minutes
**COOKING TIME: 2 hours, plus
    overnight chilling**

12 bacon slices
**About 2 lbs boneless pork
    shoulder**
About ¾ lb pig liver
1 Tbsp fennel seeds
About 1 lb bulk pork sausage
3 to 4 cloves garlic
1 Tbsp crushed red pepper
1 tsp salt
**1 tsp freshly ground black
    pepper**

WATERCRESS ROULADE WITH VEGETABLE HUMMUS

SERVES 6 TO 8 AS AN APPETIZER,
4 AS A MAIN COURSE
PREPARATION TIME: 30 minutes
COOKING TIME: 10 minutes

FOR THE ROULADE:
4 eggs
⅓ lb watercress or arugula,
very finely chopped
2 Tbsp all-purpose flour, sifted
½ tsp salt
½ tsp freshly ground black
pepper
Generous pinch of freshly
grated nutmeg

FOR THE FILLING:
5 scallions, trimmed
1 red bell pepper
2 carrots, finely shredded
1 cup prepared hummus
Salt and freshly ground black
pepper to taste

Stunningly colorful, light, and full of flavor (besides being very quick to make), this is an ideal dish for easy entertaining. Serve warm or cold, with a simple garnish of salad greens as an appetizer, or with a mixed salad and potatoes for a more substantial main course.

1 Preheat the oven to 425°F. Line a jelly-roll pan with wax paper.

2 Whisk the eggs until very thick, starting slowly and gradually increasing the speed. This will take up to 10 minutes.

3 Meanwhile, chop the watercress very finely, then add the flour, salt, pepper, and nutmeg and toss together.

4 The eggs are ready when they are very thick and pale and the wire whip leaves a thick trail in the mixture. Add the watercress and whisk briefly to combine, slowly at first and then quickly for a few seconds. Do not over mix.

5 Scrape the mixture into the prepared pan, gently level the top, and bake for 10 minutes, until set and lightly browned.

6 Turn the roulade out onto a cooling rack lined with fresh wax paper. Carefully remove the baked paper, and make a shallow cut into one end of the roulade, about ¾ inch from the edge. Roll the roulade up tightly with the paper inside to prevent it from sticking together. Leave and allow to cool for 10 minutes.

7 Finely chop the scallions and red pepper, and then mix with the carrots and hummus, seasoning to taste.

8 Unroll the roulade, remove the paper, and spread carefully with the filling. Roll again, this time using the paper on the outside just to keep the roulade firmly in shape.

9 Serve warm or cold, cut into ½-inch slices with a sharp, straight-bladed knife.

ROASTED LEMON AND SAFFRON CHICKEN LASAGNE

SERVES 6

PREPARATION TIME: 45 minutes

COOKING TIME: 1 hour and 35 minutes

FOR THE CHICKEN:

3 medium onions, each cut into 16 wedges

6 boneless chicken breasts, skin on (about 2 lbs) and cut into wide strips

Large pinch saffron strands

6 garlic cloves, peeled and cut in half lengthwise

Leaves from 4 sprigs of fresh rosemary, leaves removed and stems discarded

1 tsp sugar

2 lemons, quartered

¼ cup olive oil

Salt and freshly ground black pepper to taste

1 cup white wine

24 black olives, pitted

FOR THE PASTA:

2 cups all-purpose flour

2 eggs

1 egg yolk

Lasagne can always be counted on as a great dish for entertaining, but this version adds an element of luxury and a whole host of new flavors, colors, and textures. Slow roasting the chicken with saffron and lemons makes a huge difference to the final outcome, adding lots of flavor.

1 Preheat the oven to 400°F. Grease a large (2 to 2½ qt capacity) rectangular baking dish.

2 Place all the chicken ingredients except the white wine in a roasting pan, squeeze the lemons over them, and throw in the peel too! Mix thoroughly with your hands. Bake in the oven for 15 minutes and then add the wine, shaking the pan carefully to distribute the ingredients. Cook for another 25 minutes, shaking the tray once again during that time to ensure even cooking. Remove from the oven and allow to cool until needed. Reduce the oven temperature to 350°F.

3 Meanwhile, make the pasta. Combine the pasta ingredients with the dough hook at medium speed until they begin to form a ball. Bring the dough together with your hands.

4 Run the dough through the pasta roller on setting 1 a minimum of 15 times. Each time fold the dough back on itself before feeding it through the rollers again. When smooth and almost leathery to the touch, cut into four and increase to setting 2 and run each piece through again. Repeat this process and gradually ascend the settings to number 4. Lay the four lengths out onto a lightly floured surface and cut into about sixteen 4-inch wide rectangles.

5 Bring a large pan of salted water to a boil. Fill a bowl or the sink with cold water and lay a clean dish towel on the counter next to it. Drop the lasagne sheets into the boiling water three at a time and cook for about 30 seconds, then remove them using a slotted spoon and immediately drop them into the cold water to cool rapidly. Continue this process until all the lasagne sheets are cooked and cooled. Carefully lay each sheet on the dish towel, making sure they do not overlap. Lay another clean dish towel over the top and continue the process, finishing with another dish towel to prevent the pasta from drying

out. Leave until needed. The pasta will remain in reasonable condition like this for a few hours, but is undoubtedly better if used as soon as possible.

6 Make the béchamel sauce. Melt the butter for the sauce in a medium saucepan and then add the flour. Stir for two minutes, then gradually stir in the warm milk and continue stirring until the mixture thickens and bubbles slightly. Remove from the heat, season to taste with salt and white pepper, and mustard.

7 To assemble the lasagne, spread half the chicken mixture over the base of the prepared baking dish and scatter with 12 olives. Layer half the pasta evenly over the meat and top with half the sauce. Then repeat the process finishing with a scattering of Parmesan cheese and dot with the diced butter. Bake for 45 minutes or until golden brown all over. Serve with a green salad or vegetables.

FOR THE BÉCHAMEL SAUCE:
2 oz (½ stick) butter
2 heaping Tbsp all-purpose flour
2½ cups warmed milk
Salt and white pepper to
1 tsp dried mustard
24 pitted black olives
½ cup Parmesan cheese
1 oz (¼ stick) butter, diced

SPICY LEEK AND SQUASH PATÉ

A vivid orange color when made with butternut squash, this dip is a light appetizer with toast or vegetable crudités, or it can be served with a salad as a simple lunch. We find it to be a perfect late summer dish.

1 Slice the squash using the Rotor Slicer/Shredder, catching the pieces in a colander or steamer basket. Steam until tender, about 15 minutes. Alternatively, cook the squash with a tablespoon or two of water in the microwave for about five minutes on high. Allow to cool.

2 Slice the leek in the same way. Heat the oil in a skillet, add the leek, dried mustard, and cayenne, and cook slowly for four to five minutes, until the leek is soft but not browned. Allow the leek to cool.

3 Beat the squash until smooth in the mixer bowl using the flat beater. Add the cream cheese and beat again, adding plenty of salt and pepper.

4 Finally, add the leeks and beat them into the mixture. Season to taste with salt and pepper again and then transfer to a serving dish. Chill for about 30 minutes, but do not serve too cold or you will inhibit the flavor of the dish. Garnish with chopped parsley.

SERVES 6
PREPARATION TIME: 45 minutes, including cooling time
CHILLING TIME: 30 minutes

1 lb peeled and seeded squash, such as butternut
1 large leek (about ½ lb), trimmed
2 Tbsp olive oil
½ tsp dried mustard
½ tsp cayenne pepper or chili powder
1 cup cream cheese
Salt and freshly ground black pepper to taste
Freshly chopped parsley for garnishing

WARM GOAT CHEESE AND PARSNIP SOUFFLÉS

This is comfort food at its most glamorous! Here we unite two very distinctive flavors that act surprisingly well together. These soufflés are an ideal start to a meal, but just as good for entertaining as a lighter main course option.

1 Shred the parsnip using the coarse shredding cone of the Rotor Slicer/Shredder, then steam in a covered steamer for five to ten minutes, or until soft. Remove and pat dry on paper towels. Mash well and set aside.

2 Preheat the oven to 400°F. Grease six small pudding molds or ramekins (about 6 oz each) and dust the insides with grated Parmesan cheese, shaking away any excess.

3 Combine the butter, flour, and milk in a small saucepan and whisk continuously over a low heat until the mixture thickens. Remove from the heat and stir in the parsnip, egg yolks, goat's cheese, and spices. Season to taste with salt and pepper.

4 Using the wire whip, whisk the egg whites until soft peaks form, and then carefully fold into the parsnip mixture until just combined.

5 Divide the mixture evenly between the prepared molds, sprinkle with the remaining Parmesan cheese, and bake for 20 minutes or until risen and golden in color. Allow to cool for five minutes, by which time the soufflés will have dropped slightly. Use a knife to loosen the edges and turn out onto plates, bottom side up. Serve with mixed baby greens.

SERVES 6
PREPARATION TIME: 30 minutes
COOKING TIME: 20 minutes

2 large parsnips (about ½ lb), peeled
1 oz Parmesan cheese, finely grated
2 oz (½ stick) butter, diced
⅓ cup all-purpose flour
1 cup milk
3 eggs, separated
3½ oz soft goat cheese, chopped
Pinch of freshly grated nutmeg
Pinch of paprika
Salt and freshly ground black pepper to taste

CHEESE, APPLE, AND ZUCCHINI FONDUE

The thing that deters most people from preparing a cheese fondue for a dinner party is grating the cheese. Well, your Rotor Slicer/Shredder will make short work of that. We have often found cheese fondues to be too rich, but the addition of chile peppers, apple, and zucchini makes a much lighter dish. Use mild to medium hot chiles, according to your tastes.

1 Attach the Rotor Slicer/Shredder to your mixer with the fine shredding cone in place. Shred the shallots and chiles into a large saucepan, then change to the coarse shredder cone. Shred the zucchini and apple and add them to the pan with the white wine and lemon juice. Bring to a boil and cook for a minute or so. Remove from the heat.

2 Shred the cheeses straight into the saucepan and stir well. Return to the heat and cook slowly until the cheese has melted, stirring constantly.

3 Blend the cornstarch with a little water or more wine, add it to the pan, and cook for another three to four minutes until bubbling and thick. Season to taste with salt and pepper.

4 Pour the fondue into a fondue pot or a warmed serving dish set on a heated tray or over an appropriate burner. Dip chunks of crusty bread, carrot, or apple into the pan on long handled forks to scoop up the cheese.

COOK'S TIP: The zucchini and apple in the fondue really mask the richness of the dish, making it ideal for informal entertaining.
If the fondue cools and starts to set, reheat it gently, stirring constantly.

SERVES 6
PREPARATION TIME: 10 minutes
COOKING TIME: about 10 minutes

2 shallots
I red chile
I green chile
I zucchini, trimmed
I crisp dessert apple, quartered and cored (peel left on)
1½ cups dry white wine or hard cider
Juice of half a lemon
1⅓ lb Swiss cheese, preferably Emmentaler and Gruyère mixed
2 Tbsp cornstarch
Salt and freshly ground black pepper to taste
Chunks of crusty bread, carrots, apple, or other vegetables for dipping

EFFORTLESS DESSERTS

Some people love to make desserts and others don't think twice about buying a fruit tart to finish a meal. We have chosen a selection of our favorite flavors (you'll notice that we love chocolate!) and built a group of recipes around them. Some are quick, others require a certain amount of fiddling, but all are utterly delicious and couldn't be easier to do with a mixer.

LEMONGRASS AND LIME MOUSSE

SERVES 4

PREPARATION TIME: 1½ to 2½ hours, including chilling time

COOKING TIME: about 10 minutes

2 lemongrass stalks, tough outer layers removed

¼ cup water

2 eggs, separated (see note, page 4)

½ cup superfine sugar

Grated zest of 1 lime, plus more for garnishing

Juice of 1½ limes

1 cup heavy cream

¼-oz packet granulated gelatin

This mousse has a wonderfully delicate flavor and provides a light, clean finish to a meal.

1 Using a rolling pin, thoroughly crush the lemongrass to release its flavor. Place in a saucepan, cover with water, and simmer for 10 minutes. Allow to cool in the pan.

2 Meanwhile, using the wire whip, whisk the egg yolk with the sugar on the fastest speed setting until you have a thick, pale mixture. Add the lime zest, lime juice, and heavy cream and briefly whisk again.

3 When cool, remove the lemongrass from the pan and discard. Reheat until almost boiling, then sprinkle the gelatin over the liquid, remove from the heat and stir until the gelatin has dissolved completely. Allow to cool slightly, and then with the mixer running at medium speed, slowly pour the gelatin onto the egg mixture until thoroughly combined. Transfer to another bowl and set aside.

4 Wash the whisk and bowl thoroughly before whisking the egg whites until firm. Add to the mixture in the reserved bowl and fold in until just combined.

5 Pour into four individual serving dishes and refrigerate for one to two hours. Sprinkle with lime zest to serve.

BAKED RICOTTA CHEESECAKE SCENTED WITH ORANGE AND CARDAMOM

SERVES 6 TO 8
PREPARATION TIME: 25 minutes
COOKING TIME: 1 hour

FOR THE BASE:
⅓ cup self-rising flour
½ tsp baking powder
2 oz (½ stick) butter
¼ cup superfine sugar
1 egg

FOR THE FILLING:
1 lb whole milk ricotta cheese
1⅓ cups superfine sugar
½ cup heavy cream
4 eggs, separated
1 medium orange
6 cardamom pods
¼ tsp salt

Orange zest and chopped
   pistachio nuts for garnishing

This cheesecake is amazing — a smooth orange cream with the unique texture of ricotta cheese, combined with the occasional hint of cardamom. Yum!

1 Preheat the oven to 325°F. Grease and line the base of a 9-inch springform pan with wax paper.

2 Make the base. Sift the flour and baking powder into the mixer bowl, add the butter, sugar, and egg, and beat together at medium speed for two to three minutes, or until you can no longer hear the graininess of the sugar scraping against the bowl. The mixture should be light and pale. Spread it evenly over the bottom of the prepared pan.

3 To make the filling, use the flat beater at medium speed to combine the ricotta and sugar until smooth. Then, beat in the heavy cream and four egg yolks a little at a time. Mix thoroughly between each addition. Transfer to another bowl and refrigerate until needed.

4 Quarter the orange and remove any seeds. Then, using the Rotor Slicer/ Shredder with the fine shredding cone, shred the whole orange and the cardamom pods. Stir into the ricotta mixture and set aside.

5 Using the wire whip and a clean bowl, whisk two egg whites with the salt until they stand in firm peaks. Gently fold the whites into the ricotta mixture. Pour over the base in the prepared pan and level off.

6 Bake in the oven for about one hour or until just set and golden in color. A skewer inserted into the center should come out clean. Turn off the heat but leave the cheesecake in the oven with the door slightly ajar for another 30 minutes, then remove from the oven and allow to cool completely. This stage is most important to prevent the cake from sinking in the middle.

7 To serve, carefully release the sides of the pan and transfer to a serving plate. Decorate with orange zest and a scattering of pistachio nuts.

CLASSIC APPLE PIE

You can't beat classic apple pie served either with custard, whipped cream, or ice cream! You can count on this recipe for easy entertaining time and again.

1 Preheat the oven to 400°F. Grease a deep 9-inch pie plate.

2 Make the pastry. Sift the flour and salt into the mixer bowl. Add the butter and shortening and combine using the flat beater at slow speed until the mixture resembles breadcrumbs. Add the egg and then the water a spoonful at a time (you may not need it all) until the mixture comes together as a dough. Cover in plastic wrap and refrigerate for about 30 minutes.

3 Roll out two thirds of the pastry to about a ¼-inch thickness and line the pie plate with it, being careful to push the pastry into the edges. Roll out the remaining pastry for the lid of the pie and set aside.

4 Peel, core, and slice the apples into a large bowl. Add the remaining ingredients and mix well. Pour into the lined pie plate. Moisten the edges with water or milk and cover with the pastry lid, pressing down the edges to seal. Cut two small slits in the top of the pie to allow steam to escape, and sprinkle generously with superfine sugar. Bake for 10 minutes before lowering the temperature to 360°F and cooking for another 30 minutes or until it is a rich golden color. Serve hot or cold.

SERVES 6 TO 8
PREPARATION TIME: 50 minutes
COOKING TIME: 40 minutes

FOR THE PASTRY:
3¾ cups all-purpose flour
Pinch of salt
¼ lb (1 stick) butter
¼ lb (1 stick) vegetable shortening
1 egg, beaten
4 to 6 Tbsp cold water

FOR THE FILLING:
2 lbs cooking apples
Zest and juice of 1 lemon
½ cup superfine sugar
2 tsp cinnamon
½ tsp freshly grated nutmeg

Superfine sugar for topping

BANOFFEE MERINGUE GATEAU

'Banoffee' is the fun way to describe the heavenly combination of toffee and bananas. This dessert is such a success when entertaining. Not only does it taste amazing and wonderfully naughty, it also looks great with its sumptuous layers and impressive height.

1 Preheat the oven to 275°F. Line the base of two ungreased 7-inch baking pans with wax paper.

2 First, make the meringue. Using the wire whip, whisk the egg whites with the salt until stiff, then with the motor running at slow speed, add the sugar a teaspoonful at a time. Add the remaining meringue ingredients and combine. Divide the mixture between the two pans and level the surface of each one. Bake on the same shelf, just below the center of the oven, for about 1½ hours. When the meringue is cooked and firm to the touch, lay a dish towel on a wire rack and turn out each meringue. Remove the wax paper.

3 When the meringue is cool, whisk the heavy cream until it just begins to thicken. Slice the bananas and cover with lemon juice to prevent them from going brown. Then, begin to assemble the gateau. Take one meringue and place it in the center of a serving plate. Spoon half of the dulce de leche onto the meringue and spread out evenly. Scatter half the banana slices, followed by half the cream and some grated chocolate. Put the other meringue on top and repeat the process with the remaining ingredients. Finish with a generous amount of grated chocolate and refrigerate until needed.

COOK'S TIP: If you are unable to find Dulce de leche (an Argentinean caramel spread) simmer an unopened can of condensed milk in water for about 3 hours instead. Be very careful when doing this, however. Follow the manufacturer instructions and never attempt this if the can has a ring pull device.

SERVES 6 TO 8
PREPARATION TIME: 25 minutes
COOKING TIME: 1½ hours

FOR THE MERINGUE:
4 egg whites
Pinch of salt
¾ cup superfine sugar
1 tsp vanilla extract
1 tsp white wine vinegar
2 level Tbsp cornstarch
¼ cup chopped roasted hazelnuts

FOR THE FILLING:
1¼ cups heavy cream
3 large bananas
Juice of half a lemon
2 cups Dulce de leche (Banoffee Toffee)
1 ¾ oz good quality dark chocolate, grated (minimum 70% cocoa solids)

INDIVIDUAL
MARMALADE DESSERTS

MAKES 6 INDIVIDUAL DESSERTS
PREPARATION TIME: 15 minutes
COOKING TIME: 20 to 25
  minutes

6 Tbsp orange marmalade
1 cup self-rising flour
½ cup superfine sugar
¼ lb (1 stick) butter, softened

This recipe uses the easy, all-in-one cake method to produce delicate individual desserts with no fuss and at very little cost. You will need six small molds or ramekins (about 6 ounces each) and six lightly greased 6-inch squares of aluminum foil.

1 Preheat the oven to 350°F. Grease the molds thoroughly and put 1 tablespoon of marmalade into the bottom of each one.
2 Sift the flour into the mixer bowl and add all the other ingredients. Combine using the flat beater until well mixed and smooth.

3 Spoon the mixture equally into the prepared molds and level the surface of each one. Cover each mold with a square of greased foil and place on a cookie sheet. Bake for about 20 to 25 minutes or until the sponge bounces back when pressed lightly.

4 Loosen the edges of each dessert with a knife and then turn out onto individual plates. Serve immediately with softly whipped cream.

....

COOK'S TIP: When serving, try flavoring the softly whipped cream with Drambuie or Cointreau and a little sifted confectioners' sugar to taste.

2 eggs, beaten
1 tsp ground ginger
Softly whipped cream for serving

LEMON IMPOSSIBLE DESSERT

Far from being "impossible" to make, this dessert is so named because it seems impossible that the unusual looking batter could come out of the oven as a light sponge floating on a delicious puddle of lemon sauce. This recipe has been a family favorite for years.

....

1 Preheat the oven to 350°F. Grease a deep ovenproof dish (about 4 cups capacity). Stand this in a roasting pan.

2 Using the wire whip, mix the egg yolks with the sugar until light and creamy, then add the milk, flour, lemon zest, and lemon juice and whisk until well combined. The mixture will probably separate and look as if something has gone horribly wrong! But don't worry, simply transfer to a separate bowl and set aside.

3 Thoroughly wash and dry the mixing bowl before whisking the whites and salt together until stiff. Fold into the lemon mixture with a metal spoon.

4 Transfer the mixture to the prepared dish, and then pour hot water into the roasting tray to come half way up the side of the dish. Bake for about 50 minutes or until risen and lightly golden. Serve immediately.

SERVES 4
PREPARATION TIME: 20 minutes
COOKING TIME: 50 minutes

3 eggs, separated
⅓ cup superfine sugar
¾ cup milk
1 Tbsp self-rising flour, sifted
Grated zest and juice of 2 large lemons
Pinch of salt
Hot water (see method)

BAILEYS CHOCOLATE TART

This decadent dessert is always a showstopper, whether entertaining formally or at a relaxed lunch, morning coffee, or afternoon tea! This is for serious chocoholics and Baileys fans only!

....

1 Make the pastry. Sift the flour, confectioners' sugar, cocoa, and salt into the mixer bowl and combine with the butter using the flat beater at the slowest speed until the mixture resembles breadcrumbs. Add the yolk and mix until it begins to come together. Gather the dough into a ball with your hands and cover with plastic wrap. Refrigerate for 30 minutes.

2 Preheat the oven to 325°F. Grease a 9-inch tart pan that has a removable bottom. On a lightly floured surface, roll the pastry out to about ¼-inch thickness. Lay the pastry in the pan and press firmly into the edges. Carefully line the pastry with aluminum foil or wax paper. Weigh the tart down with pie weights, dried beans, or rice and bake for 30 minutes. Remove the tart from the oven, remove the beans and foil or paper, and allow to cool in the pan on a wire rack.

3 While the pastry case is cooling, make the filling. Whisk the heavy cream until it just begins to thicken. Melt the milk chocolate by placing it in the microwave in a microwave-safe bowl on high power for 1½ minutes. Remove and stir to dissolve any lumps. Add the Baileys to the melted chocolate and stir thoroughly. The mixture will become very thick, but don't worry; simply add a spoon of the whipped cream and mix together. Continue this process until you have about 2 tablespoons of whipped cream remaining. Fold the remaining cream into the chocolate, but this time, do not combine thoroughly so you are left with a marbled effect.

4 When the pastry is cool, melt the dark chocolate and use a pastry brush to "paint" the inside of the pastry case with it. Allow this chocolate to set, about two to five minutes, and then pour the filling into the pastry case, smooth the surface. Refrigerate for at least one hour or until needed. Serve dusted with cocoa powder and accompanied by fruit, such as sliced oranges or raspberries (to help cut through the richness of the dessert).

SERVES 6 TO 8

PREPARATION TIME: 1 hour and 45 minutes, including chilling time

COOKING TIME: 30 minutes

FOR THE PASTRY:
- **1 cup all-purpose flour**
- **½ cup confectioners' sugar**
- **1 Tbsp cocoa powder, plus extra for dusting**
- **½ tsp salt**
- **¼ lb (1 stick) butter, chilled and diced**
- **1 egg yolk**

FOR THE FILLING:
- **1¼ cups heavy cream**
- **7 oz luxury milk chocolate**
- **2 Tbsp Baileys Original Irish Cream® or other Irish cream liqueur (or to taste!)**
- **1 oz luxury dark chocolate (minimum 70% cocoa solids)**

BAKED FIG AND MASCARPONE TART WITH WALNUT PRALINE

This fantastic dessert will keep guests coming back for more! It combines a crisp pâte sucrée base (traditional French sweet pastry), soft mascarpone custard with dried figs, and a seriously crunchy walnut praline topping. There's a lot going on, but the flavors and textures marry perfectly.

SERVES 6 TO 8

PREPARATION TIME: 40 minutes, plus 2 to 12 hours for chilling

COOKING TIME: 1 hour

FOR THE PÂTE SUCRÉE:

1½ cups all-purpose flour, sifted

1 level Tbsp superfine sugar

Pinch of salt

¼ lb (1 stick) butter, chilled and diced

1 egg, beaten

FOR THE PRALINE:

½ cup superfine sugar

¼ cup water

¾ cup walnut pieces

FOR THE FILLING:

5 dried figs, sliced

14 oz mascarpone cheese

2 oz (½ stick) unsalted butter, softened

¼ cup superfine sugar

3 eggs

1 tsp grated lemon zest

Softly whipped cream for serving

1 Make the pastry. Sift the flour, sugar, and salt into the mixer bowl and combine using the flat beater. Then add the butter and mix on a slow speed until the mixture resembles breadcrumbs. Add the egg and continue mixing until the dough comes together. Cover it in plastic wrap and refrigerate for 30 minutes.

2 Meanwhile, make the walnut praline. Grease a cookie sheet (that has sides) and set aside. In a small pan over low heat, combine the sugar with the water until the sugar dissolves. Increase the heat and boil the syrup without stirring until it becomes a light caramel color. This will take about three to five minutes. Add the nuts and stir gently to coat evenly, then spoon onto the prepared cookie sheet and make level with the back of the spoon. Set aside to cool completely, by which time the mixture will have solidified. Using a knife, shatter or roughly chop the praline into about ½-inch shards.

3 Preheat the oven to 350°F. Grease a 9-inch tart pan that has a removable bottom. Remove the pastry from the refrigerator and roll out on a lightly floured surface to about ¼-inch thickness. Line the prepared pan with the pastry, pinching the edges with thumb and forefinger to make it look more attractive. Line with aluminum foil or wax paper and weigh down with pie weights, dried beans, or rice. Bake for 10 minutes, then remove the weights and the foil or paper and bake for another 10 minutes. Remove from the oven and allow to cool in the pan on a wire rack. Reduce the temperature to 325°F.

4 While the pastry is baking, make the filling. Combine the mascarpone cheese, butter, and sugar using the flat beater. When the mixture is smooth, add the eggs and lemon zest and mix again. Set aside in a cool place.

5 When the pastry is cool, scatter the sliced figs over the base and pour the mascarpone mixture over the top. Bake for 40 minutes, or until the custard has set. Remove from the oven and immediately sprinkle with the walnut praline and allow to cool in the pan for at least two hours, but preferably about 12 hours. Remove from the pan, slice, and serve with lightly whipped cream.

CHOCOLATE AND ALMOND TORTE

This flourless torte is surprisingly light. Use a really good quality chocolate with at least 70% cocoa solids for a slightly bitter, light result. Serve with whipped cream or sour cream – or a toffee ice cream – and decorate with chocolate curls or soft seasonal fruits.

SERVES 8 TO 10

PREPARATION TIME: 25 to 30 minutes

COOKING TIME: 40 minutes

¼ lb (1 stick) unsalted butter

5½ oz good quality dark chocolate, broken into small pieces

5 eggs, separated

1¾ cups ground almonds

¾ cup light brown sugar, or light Muscavado sugar if available

Confectioners' sugar for dusting

1 Preheat the oven to 325°F. Butter and line the base of a 9-inch springform pan with wax paper.

2 Melt the butter and chocolate in a large bowl over a pan of hot water, or heat in the microwave for two to three minutes. Cool slightly.

3 Whisk the egg whites, gradually increasing the speed, until they form stiff peaks. Meanwhile, add the egg yolks, almonds, and brown sugar to the chocolate and mix well.

4 Lightly and gently fold the egg whites into the chocolate in three batches with a large metal spoon. Scrape the mixture into the prepared pan, gently tapping the sides to level the top, and bake for 35 to 40 minutes until set. Allow the torte to cool in the pan.

5 Dust with confectioners' sugar before slicing and serving.

COOK'S TIP: Always add the egg whites to the chocolate mixture, and not the other way around, or the resulting torte will be heavy.

COFFEE CREAM ÉCLAIRS

MAKES ABOUT 12 ÉCLAIRS
PREPARATION TIME: 20 minutes
COOKING TIME: 30 minutes

FOR THE PASTY:
1 cup water
2 oz (½ stick) butter
1 cup all-purpose flour (sifted
    into a square of parchment
    paper)
Pinch of salt
1 egg yolk, beaten
2 whole eggs, beaten

FOR THE ICING:
1 cup confectioners' sugar
1 Tbsp instant coffee granules
1 Tbsp hot water

FOR THE FILLING:
1 cup heavy cream
1 Tbsp Tía Maria (optional)

It seems everybody loves cream éclairs! These are topped with coffee icing, and we give you the option of making a Tía Maria cream filling. Your mixer takes all the effort out of making choux pastry and produces fabulous results.

1 Preheat the oven to 425°F and lightly grease a cookie sheet.

2 Make the choux pastry. Melt the butter in the water in a saucepan over a low heat, then bring to a rapid boil. Add the flour and beat quickly with a wooden spoon until mixed, then pour into the mixer bowl and beat on a medium speed for one minute, or until the mixture leaves the sides of the bowl cleanly. Allow to cool for a few minutes. Gradually add the beaten egg, mixing slowly at first, and then a little faster. The mixture should hold its shape, so only add as much of the egg as is necessary.

3 Fill a pastry bag fitted with a ¾-inch plain tip with the pastry mixture and pipe twelve 4-inch lengths onto the prepared cookie sheet. Bake for 10 minutes, then lower the oven temperature to 350°F and bake for another 15 minutes or until risen and golden. Remove from the oven and immediately cut along the length of each éclair to let the steam escape. There should not be any moist dough remaining in the center of the éclairs. If there is, return them to the oven (which has been switched off) for about two minutes, by which time they should be cooked through. Allow to cool completely on a wire rack.

4 While the éclairs are cooling, make the icing by combining the ingredients and mixing thoroughly. Allow to stand until needed.

5 For the filling, whisk the heavy cream until firm, then add the Tía Maria if you are using it. Whisk again to combine. When the pastry is cool, fill a pastry bag (fitted with the same size tip as before) with the whipped cream and neatly fill each éclair. Top each one with about 1 to 2 teaspoons of icing and set aside to set before serving.

PUMPKIN PIE

Pumpkin pie is a classic, but here it is given a slight twist with the addition of sour cream to the filling and ground ginger to the pastry base.

1 Grease a 9-inch loose bottomed fluted pie plate.

2 Make the pastry. Sift the flour, salt, and ginger into the mixer bowl. Add the butter and using the flat beater at slow speed, combine until the mixture resembles breadcrumbs. Add enough cold water, a spoonful at a time, to make a firm dough. Bring the dough together with your hands, and on a lightly floured surface, roll out to about ¼-inch thickness. Line the prepared pan with the pastry, pinching the edges with thumb and forefinger to make it look more attractive. Refrigerate for 30 minutes.

3 Meanwhile, make the filling. Preheat the oven to 400°F. Using the flat beater, purée the cooked pumpkin, then add the brown sugar, salt, and spices and mix again before adding the remaining ingredients and combining thoroughly. The filling should be smooth and runny in consistency.

4 Pour the filling into the chilled pastry case and bake for 15 minutes before lowering the temperature to 350°F. Cook for another 45 minutes or until just set; the tip of a knife inserted into the center of the pie should come out clean. Cool the pie for at least an hour before serving with whipped cream or ice cream.

COOK'S TIP: For this recipe, we use a pumpkin weighing about 1 pound. Peel it, remove the seeds, and cut it into rough cubes. Place it in a bowl with 2 tablespoons of water, cover, and cook in the microwave for about 10 minutes, or until soft. Alternatively, you can steam the peeled and seeded pumpkin in a covered steamer over a pan of boiling water.

SERVES 6 TO 8
PREPARATION TIME: 40 minutes
COOKING TIME: 60 minutes

FOR THE PASTRY:
1½ cups all-purpose flour
½ tsp salt
1 tsp ground ginger
¼ lb (1 stick) butter, chilled and diced
3 to 4 Tbsp cold water

FOR THE FILLING:
2 cups cooked pumpkin (see Cook's tip below)
¾ cup light brown sugar
Pinch of salt
2 tsp cinnamon
½ tsp freshly grated nutmeg
3 eggs, beaten
½ cup sour cream
½ cup milk

CRANACHAN CREAM

This traditional Scottish dessert looks and tastes great. An added advantage with this recipe is that it can be made quickly and easily and then left in the refrigerator for up to six hours before being served.

1 Place the oatmeal in a baking pan and toast under a preheated broiler for three to five minutes, or until golden. Shake the pan frequently to ensure that the oatmeal browns evenly. Remove from the pan and set aside.

2 Whip the cream with the wire whip just until it begins to thicken, then add the sugar and whisky and briefly whisk to combine.

3 Using four 8½ oz glasses (or one large glass serving dish) begin layering the ingredients by putting a spoonful of cream into each one. Follow this with a few raspberries and a scattering of oatmeal. Continue this process to create haphazard layers, which look (and possibly taste) better. Finish with a dusting of oatmeal and garnish with three perfect raspberries per serving. Refrigerate until needed.

COOK'S TIP: Don't be tempted to whip the cream too much, because the texture of the dessert will become dry.

SERVES 4
PREPARATION TIME: 20 minutes
COOKING TIME: 3 to 5 minutes

½ **cup oatmeal**
1 **cups heavy cream**
1 **heaping Tbsp superfine sugar**
1 **to 2 Tbsp whisky (to taste)**
1½ **cups fresh raspberries, hulled, with extra for garnishing**

GRAPEFRUIT SORBET WITH VERMOUTH

SERVES 6 TO 8

PREPARATION TIME: about
1 hour and 20 minutes,
   including cooling and
   chilling time

FREEZING TIME: 3 to 4 hours
   without an ice cream
   machine, 30 minutes with

3 grapefruits, grated and
   juiced
2 cinnamon sticks
1 cup superfine sugar
2 egg whites
  (see note, page 4)
Vermouth to serve (extra dry,
   or to taste)

Sorbet is really refreshing at the end of a meal, and this is one of the best recipes that we have come across. Creamy white in color, it needs just a generous splash of vermouth poured over it before serving.

1 Measure the grapefruit juice and bring it up to 3 cups with as much water as is necessary. Place in a pan with the grated rind and cinnamon sticks and bring to a boil. Cover and leave for five minutes, then discard the cinnamon sticks. Stir in the sugar to dissolve, then strain the mixture into a bowl. Allow to cool, then chill for one hour.

2 Whisk the egg whites in the mixer bowl until white and fluffy but not stiff. Pour in the chilled grapefruit mixture and continue whisking until well combined. Pour into an ice cream maker and freeze-churn until ready to serve. Alternatively, pour into a suitable plastic container and freeze for three to four hours, stirring vigorously at least twice.

3 Serve in scoops with a good splash of vermouth.

COOK'S TIP: Allow the sorbet to stand in the refrigerator for 20 to 30 minutes or so before serving if it has been frozen solid. If it is melting unevenly, pour into the mixer bowl and mix with the flat beater to make it smooth. Serve immediately, or freeze again until scoopable.

RHUBARB AND ORANGE PAVLOVA

Of course you can use any fruit you like on a Pavlova, but rhubarb and orange is unusual and quite good! Your mixer makes the perfect meringue – just remember to add the sugar slowly, a small spoonful at a time.

....

1 Preheat the oven to 325°F. Line a cookie sheet with wax paper, draw a 10-inch circle on the paper, and sprinkle with a little superfine sugar.

2 Whisk the egg whites with the salt until stiff. Start slowly and gradually increase the speed of your mixer.

3 With the motor still running, whisk in the sugar, a small spoonful at a time. This will not take as long as you think, and it is well worth the extra time to incorporate the sugar slowly. Mix the cream of tartar and the cornstarch in with the last of the sugar and add to the egg whites, then add the vanilla extract and vinegar. The resulting meringue should be stiff, thick, and glossy.

4 Pile the meringue onto the prepared baking sheet and spread it out to cover the marked circle. Bake for two hours, or two and a half hours if you like your meringue crisp through to the middle. Allow to cool.

5 Cut the rhubarb into 2-inch lengths and place in a pan with the water and sugar. Cover and cook slowly for 10 minutes, until just tender. Grate the zest from the oranges into the pan, then roughly chop the flesh, mix into the pan and then remove from the heat. Allow to cool.

6 Place the meringue on a serving platter. Whisk the heavy cream until it forms soft peaks and pile onto the center of the cooked meringue. Top with the rhubarb and orange mixture, and spoon some of the juices over each serving.

SERVES 6 to 8
PREPARATION TIME: 30 minutes
COOKING TIME: 2 to 2 ½ hours

4 egg whites
  (see note, page 4)
Pinch of salt
1 cup superfine sugar, plus
  some for sprinkling
½ tsp cream of tartar
1 Tbsp cornstarch
½ tsp vanilla extract
1 tsp white wine vinegar
¾ lb cleaned rhubarb
4 Tbsp water
4 Tbsp sugar
2 oranges
1 to 1¼ cups heavy cream

MANGO MERINGUE ROULADE

SERVES 8 TO 10

PREPARATION TIME: 30 minutes
   plus chilling time

COOKING TIME: 20 to 25
   minutes

5 egg whites (save the yolks to
   make your own fruit curd)
   (see note, page 4)
1 cup superfine sugar
⅓ cup dried flaked coconut
1 cup heavy cream
1 large ripe mango, peeled
   and diced
Passion fruit, raspberries or
   physallis to decorate

A meringue roulade is a light but indulgent dessert and perfect any time of year with whatever fruits are in season. It's also delicious filled with whipped cream mixed with citrus curd or cheese — orange, lemon, or lime all work well. This freezes admirably.

1 Preheat the oven to 375°F. Line a jelly-roll pan (about 12 x 9 inches) with wax paper.

2 Whisk the egg whites until very stiff, starting slowly and then gradually increasing the mixer speed. Keep whisking on a high speed and add the sugar a spoonful at a time. Whisk well between each addition; the meringue will be very stiff and firm when finished. Pile it into the prepared pan and spread evenly, scattering the coconut over the smoothed surface.

3 Bake for 20 to 25 minutes, until lightly browned and firm to the touch. The meringue may have cracked a bit, but that's ok.

4 Transfer the meringue to a wire rack lined with more wax paper. Any darkly browned coconut will hopefully fall off at this stage! Remove the baked paper and allow to cool for 10 to 15 minutes.

5 Whisk the cream to form soft peaks, gradually increasing the mixer speed. Fold in the mango and any mango juice with a spoon, and then spread the cream evenly over the meringue. Make a deep incision along one of the long sides, and then roll up, using the wax paper to help. Be sure to roll firmly and tightly so the roulade will keep its shape. Chill, wrapped in the paper, for at least an hour or two before serving.

6 To serve, remove the paper and cut into slices. Arrange on a platter and decorate with seasonal fruits; passion fruit is especially delicious drizzled over each slice.

COOK'S TIP: For a slightly crisper meringue, bake at 425°F for 10 to 12 minutes, or until browned and slightly firm, then reduce the heat to 325°F and cook for another 15 to 20 minutes until "solid."

CAKES AND BAKES

This is traditionally where a mixer really comes into its own! Everyone loves a homemade cake, and we have a selection of traditional and contemporary bars for every occasion. Your mixer will cream and whisk to perfection, but remember to check out the blueprint recipes and mixing tips at the beginning of the book before you start, especially if you are a novice baker.

TROPICAL FRUIT CAKE

MAKES I LARGE CAKE
PREPARATION TIME: 30
  minutes, plus overnight
  soaking
COOKING TIME: 2 to 2¼ hours

I½ cups golden raisins
I cup raisins
¾ cup dried currants
275ml bottle Bacardi
  Breezer® (orange,
  pineapple, or watermelon)
I½ cups dried mixed tropical
  fruits
¾ cup candied cherries
I cup dried flaked coconut
¾ cup macadamia nuts,
  roughly chopped
7 oz marzipan, cut into ½-inch
  chunks
I cup all-purpose flour
½ tsp ground mace
½ tsp baking powder
Pinch of salt
2 oz (½ stick) butter, at room
  temperature
½ cup superfine sugar
½ cup light brown sugar, or
  light Muscovado sugar if
  available
2 eggs
½ tsp almond extract

This is a fabulously exotic cake, loaded with tropical fruit, coconut, and more than a touch of alcohol. It's special enough to cover with icing for a holiday or special occasion, and it's sophisticated enough to nibble, just as it is, with a cocktail by the pool.

1 Soak the golden raisins, raisins, and currants in half the Bacardi Breezer, cover, and leave overnight. Don't drink the rest of the Bacardi – you'll certainly need some of it for the recipe!

2 Snip the tropical fruits into roughly ½-inch chunks and cut the cherries in half. Add to the soaked fruits along with the coconut and macadamia nuts and mix well. Add the marzipan.

3 Preheat the oven to 325°F. Oil a 9-inch round cake pan and line the base with wax paper.

4 Sift together the flour, mace, baking powder, and salt.

5 Combine the butter and sugars in the mixing bowl with the flat beater on a low speed; there's too much sugar for the mixture to become creamy, but it will blend together. Add the eggs one at a time, slightly increasing the speed to achieve a more traditional cake-like batter, then add the almond extract and the sifted flour mixture. Beat thoroughly for one minute.

6 Add the soaked fruits and nuts, with any remaining liquid, mixing slowly to combine all the ingredients. Pile the mixture into the prepared pan, pressing down firmly; the pan will be full, but the cake hardly rises during baking.

7 Bake for about two hours, or until a dark golden color. If the cake is browning too quickly, cover with aluminum foil or wax paper. Test with a skewer inserted into the center of the cake; if it comes out clean and the fruit is no longer "singing", the cake is done. When testing for doneness, try to avoid the chunks of marzipan because it will make the skewer come out sticky.

8 Leave the cake to cool in the pan. When cold, remove the cake carefully and make lots of holes in the top and bottom with a skewer. Spoon some of the remaining Bacardi over the surface, allowing it to soak in. Don't make it too moist!

9 Wrap in foil and leave to mature for at least a couple of days – a couple of weeks is best. Serve very thick slices, as the large pieces of fruit and nut will cause the cake to crumble.

PUMPKIN, RUM, AND RAISIN CAKE

Add a little whipped cream to a piece of the cake and serve with coffee.

....

1 Soak the raisins in the rum for at least 10 minutes, the longer the better.

2 Preheat the oven to 350°F and line the base of a large loaf pan with wax paper.

3 If using freshly roasted pumpkin or squash, cut into chunks and place in the mixer bowl. Beat until smooth on a medium speed using the flat beater.

4 If using canned pumpkin, add it now. Add the margarine, brown sugar, eggs, and self-rising flour and beat together on a medium speed until thoroughly blended. Add the raisins and the rum and continue mixing for another minute.

5 Pour into the prepared pan and bake for one hour. Cool slightly in the pan, then turn out onto a wire rack to cool completely.

MAKES 1 LARGE CAKE
PREPARATION TIME: 30 minutes, or 1½ hours if roasting pumpkin
COOKING TIME: 1 hour

1 cup raisins
¼ cup dark rum
½ a 15 oz can pumpkin purée, or 7 oz (a heaping ¾ cup) cooked pumpkin or squash
6 oz (1½ sticks) margarine
1 cup light brown sugar, or light Muscovado sugar if available
2 eggs
2 cups self-rising flour

DATE AND OAT SLICE

This has long been a favorite treat — rich, filling, and ever so easy to make.

....

1 Preheat the oven to 350°F. Lightly butter an 8-inch round cake pan.

2 Cook the dates and water together gently in a pan until the dates are soft and the water slightly reduced.

3 Meanwhile, pour the melted butter into the mixer bowl, add the flour, brown sugar, and oats and mix well using the flat beater. Press half the mixture into the prepared pan, and transfer the rest to a plate and reserve until needed.

4 Pour the dates and water into the mixer bowl, add the vanilla extract, and beat until smooth. Spread the dates over the batter in the pan, then top with the remaining oat mixture.

5 Bake for 30 minutes, until lightly browned and set. Mark into slices in the pan while still warm and leave in the pan to cool. Cut into slices when almost cold. Store in an airtight container.

SERVES 8
PREPARATION TIME: 20 minutes
COOKING TIME: 30 minutes

1½ cups dried dates, roughly chopped
⅔ cup water
6 oz (1½ sticks) butter, melted
1 cup all-purpose flour
1 cup light brown sugar, or light Muscovado sugar if available
2 cups rolled oats
1 tsp vanilla extract

CRANBERRY AND ORANGE CRUMBLE CAKE

MAKES I LARGE CAKE
PREPARATION TIME: 30 minutes
COOKING TIME: about 1½ hours

2 cups fresh, or frozen
   defrosted cranberries
2 oranges, peeled and roughly
   chopped

FOR THE TOPPING:
I cup self-rising wholewheat
   flour (or I cup regular
   wholewheat flour and 2 tsp
   baking powder)
¼ lb (I stick) butter
I cup raw sugar

FOR THE CAKE:
6 oz (1½ sticks) butter
I cup light brown sugar, or
   light Muscovado sugar if
   available
3 eggs, beaten
2 cups self-rising flour
I tsp ground cinnamon

Crumble cakes are a delicious half-way point between a dessert and a cake. They are lovely warm with custard or cream, and wonderful when cold. This is an excellent cake to serve with morning coffee.

1 Preheat the oven to 350°F. Line a 9-inch springform pan with wax paper.

2 Mix together the cranberries and oranges and set aside.

3 Prepare the topping. Blend the wholewheat flour and butter on a medium speed with the flat beater until the mixture resembles lumpy breadcrumbs, then mix in the sugar. Transfer the topping to a plate.

4 Make the cake. Cream the butter and brown sugar together with the flat beater until pale in color. Gradually add the eggs, beating well after each addition; the mixture may start to curdle but keep beating. Fold in the self-rising flour and cinnamon on the lowest speed until blended. The mixture should be quite stiff.

5 Carefully spoon the cake mixture into the bottom of the prepared pan and scatter first the fruits, and then the topping, over the cake.

6 Bake for about one and a half hours, until a skewer inserted into the cake comes out clean. Allow to cool slightly in the pan and serve warm. For a traditional cake, remove from the pan to a wire rack and allow to cool completely before serving.

COOK'S TIP: Make the cake with cranberry and orange sauce when fresh fruit is not available. However, store the finished cake in the refrigerator if made with fresh fruits.

TRADITIONAL CARROT CAKE WITH CREAM CHEESE FROSTING

MAKES I LARGE CAKE
PREPARATION TIME: 20 minutes
COOKING TIME: I hour

FOR THE CARROT CAKE:
¾ cup superfine sugar
¾ cup sunflower or vegetable
  oil
2 eggs, beaten
1⅓ cups self-rising flour, sifted
I tsp pumpkin spice
½ tsp salt
½ Tbsp honey
½ lb carrots, coarsely grated
  using the Slicer & Shredder
  attachment
¼ cup walnut pieces, plus
  more for garnishing
¼ cup raisins

FOR CREAM CHEESE FROSTING:
½ cup cream cheese
I oz (¼ stick) butter, at room
  temperature
I Tbsp lemon juice
I tsp lemon zest
¾ cup confectioners' sugar

We love this recipe, as it is consistently good and so easy to make! If you prefer a round cake, use an 8-inch round cake pan.

I Preheat the oven to 325°F. Oil and line the base of a large loaf pan with wax paper.

2 Make the cake. Combine the sugar, oil, and eggs in the mixer bowl and beat until thick and pale, using the flat beater on a medium high setting. Add the flour, spice, salt, and honey, and continue to beat until blended.

3 Stir in the remaining cake ingredients, then pour the mixture into the prepared pan and bake for one hour or until a skewer inserted into the cake comes out clean. Allow to cool in the pan for about five minutes, and then turn out onto a wire rack to cool completely.

4 Make the frosting. Beat the cream cheese, butter, lemon juice, and zest together using the flat beater, then beat in the confectioners' sugar. Spread the frosting on top of the cooled cake and decorate with walnut pieces.

COOK'S TIP: You simply cannot make frosting with low-fat cream cheese; it becomes very runny and will not coat the cake. Full fat cheese is the only way!

ANGEL CAKE WITH ORANGE GLAZE

The orange glaze makes this light cake look incredibly attractive. Sifting the flour four times sounds excessive, but it is necessary for the cake to be a success.

1 Preheat the oven 375°F. Grease a 10-inch tube or Bundt pan.

2 Sift the flour four times and set aside. Use the wire whip, and whisk the egg whites with the salt and cream of tartar until soft peaks form. With the motor still running, gradually whisk the sugar into the egg whites, a teaspoon at a time. Take the time to do this slowly.

3 Fold the flour into the egg whites in three batches using a metal spoon. Work quickly and lightly. Then, add the vanilla extract. Pour into the prepared pan and bake for 35 to 40 minutes or until very lightly golden in color. Allow to cool in the pan upside down on a wire rack.

4 When completely cool, loosen the edges of the cake with a sharp knife and then turn the cake out onto a serving plate, tapping the pan to release it.

5 To make the glaze, simply combine the ingredients and mix well until smooth. Let stand for five minutes, and then pour over the top of the cake and leave in a cool place to set.

COOK'S TIP: The sifting of the flour and the cooling of the cake upside down in the pan are essential stages in making a successful Angel Cake.

MAKES I LARGE CAKE
PREPARATION TIME: 15 minutes
COOKING TIME: 35 to 40 minutes

FOR THE CAKE:
¾ cup all-purpose flour
6 egg whites
¼ tsp salt
½ tsp cream of tartar
I cup superfine sugar
2 tsp vanilla extract

FOR THE GLAZE:
Grated rind of I orange
2 Tbsp orange juice
½ cup confectioners' sugar, sifted

SPONGE SANDWICH CAKE WITH YOGURT AND RASPBERRY FILLING

This is the most traditional of cakes, and yields a wonderfully moist and springy sponge sandwich. Usually filled with jam and topped with a sprinkling of sugar, here we combine yogurt and raspberries for a fabulous treat.

MAKES I LARGE CAKE
PREPARATION TIME: 20 minutes
COOKING TIME: 20 to 25 minutes

5 oz (1¼ sticks) butter
⅔ cup superfine sugar
2 eggs, lightly beaten
I cup self-rising flour, sifted
½ tsp baking powder
About I cup plain yogurt
1½ cups fresh raspberries

1 Preheat the oven to 350°F. Lightly grease and line the base of two 7-inch round pans with wax paper.

2 Using the flat beater, beat together the butter and the sugar until pale and fluffy and you are certain that all the sugar has been dissolved. Add half the eggs to the mixture and beat again until well combined, then beat in the remaining eggs (adding a tablespoon of flour if the mixture looks as if it might curdle).

3 Add the sifted flour and baking powder to the bowl and fold in on the slowest setting until just combined. The batter should be soft and flick easily off a spoon. If necessary, fold in up to 2 tablespoons water (or raspberry liqueur if you are feeling frivolous!) to achieve this consistency.

4 Spoon into the prepared pans and bake on the same shelf in the oven to ensure even cooking, for about 20 to 25 minutes or until the sponge springs back when pressed lightly.

5 Cool for five minutes in the pans, then turn out onto a wire rack to cool completely.

6 Fold the raspberries into the yogurt and use as a filling between the two cakes, sandwiching them together.

COOK'S TIP: If you wish, you could put more of the yogurt mixture on top of the cake, too, and then decorate with more raspberries and mint leaves.

WHITE CHOCOLATE TRUFFLE CAKE

MAKES I LARGE CAKE
PREPARATION TIME: 60
   minutes, including chilling
   time for topping
COOKING TIME: 40 minutes

FOR THE CAKE:

6 oz (1½ sticks) unsalted
   butter, softened
1½ cups superfine sugar
4 eggs, beaten
1 tsp vanilla extract
2½ cups all-purpose flour
2½ tsp baking powder
½ tsp salt
1¼ cups milk
9 oz white chocolate, melted

FOR THE TRUFFLE TOPPING:

9 oz white chocolate
1 cup heavy cream
2 egg whites
   (see note, page 4)
White or dark chocolate
   shavings for decoration
   (see method)

Chocolate heaven — this cake not only tastes fabulous but looks really stunning, too. The cake is improved if, after cooling, you wrap it in plastic wrap and store overnight before topping with the truffle mixture and then serving.

1 Preheat the oven to 350°F. Grease and line the base of two round 7-inch cake pans with wax paper.

2 Beat the butter at a low speed with the flat beater to soften. Add the sugar and beat until fluffy, then add the eggs, one at a time, beating well between each addition. Add the vanilla extract. Sift the dry ingredients into the bowl in three separate stages, beating in at a low speed and adding the milk. Add the melted chocolate and mix well.

3 Divide the batter between the two pans, smooth the tops, and bake for 40 minutes or until a skewer inserted into the middle of each cake comes out clean. Cool in the pans for 10 minutes and then turn out onto a wire rack to cool completely.

4 To make the topping, melt the chocolate and allow to cool slightly before adding the cream and stirring thoroughly. Whisk the whites in the mixer, using the wire whip, until firm peaks form, and then fold the egg whites into the chocolate mixture. Spread half the mixture onto one of the cakes, then top with the other cake and spread the remaining mixture over the top and sides of the cake. Complete with white and/or dark chocolate shavings that can be made using the fine shredding cone of the Rotor Slicer/Shredder attachment. Chill for at least half an hour before serving.

SERIOUSLY LEMONY LEMON BARS

These fabulous recipe uses the all-in-one cake method, so it's very quick and easy to make. The things to remember are that the butter must be very soft, and that extra baking powder is needed because air is not beaten into the mixture during an initial creaming process. As a dessert, it is better eaten after about 12 hours, and will keep well for several days in a cool place. It also freezes well.

....

1 Preheat the oven to 350°F. Grease a rectangular baking pan (13 x 9 x 2 inches).

2 Make the pastry base. Combine the flour and salt in the mixer bowl, and then blend in the butter using the flat beater on a slow speed until the mixture resembles fine breadcrumbs. Add the sugar and eggs gradually to form a dough.

3 Transfer the pastry to a floured surface and roll out to fit the prepared pan, pressing the pastry against the edges of the pan. Chill in the refrigerator while you continue with the recipe.

4 Make the lemon sponge cake. Put all the cake ingredients except for the zest, juice, and lemon curd into the mixer bowl and combine on a medium speed. Add the zest and juice and mix in quickly.

5 Spread the lemon curd evenly over the chilled pastry, then spread the cake mixture over and smooth the top.

6 Bake for about 40 minutes until risen and golden brown. The sponge should spring back when pressed gently. Leave in the pan to cool, preferably overnight, and then cut into fingers.

MAKES ABOUT 25 LARGE SLICES
PREPARATION TIME: 35 minutes
COOKING TIME: 40 minutes

FOR SWEET PASTRY BASE:
1½ cups all-purpose flour, sifted
Pinch of salt
6 oz (1½ sticks) butter, chilled and cut into cubes
1 Tbsp superfine sugar
2 eggs, beaten

FOR LEMON SPONGE CAKE:
2 cups self-rising flour, sifted
1 tsp baking powder
1 cup superfine sugar
½ lb (2 sticks) butter, very soft
4 eggs, beaten
Grated zest of 1 lemon
2 Tbsp lemon juice
1 cup prepared lemon curd

CHOCA-MOCHA COLA CAKE

MAKES 1 LARGE CAKE
PREPARATION TIME: 20 minutes
COOKING TIME: 40 minutes

FOR THE CAKE:
1¾ cups self-rising flour
1 cup superfine sugar
¼ tsp baking soda
½ lb (2 sticks) butter
½ cup cocoa powder
¾ cup cola
2 Tbsp instant coffee granules
½ cup milk
1 egg, beaten
1 tsp vanilla extract

FOR THE TOPPING:
½ cup cocoa powder, sifted
1 Tbsp light corn syrup, or
    golden syrup if available
1 oz (¼ stick) butter
½ cup cola
1 Tbsp instant coffee granules

It is difficult to imagine this cake without tasting it first, but it is a wonderfully moist, rich chocolate sponge with an incredible topping. It is great served slightly warm with ice cream!

1 Preheat the oven to 350°F. Grease a 10-inch springform pan.

2 Make the cake. In the mixer bowl, combine the flour, sugar, and baking soda using the flat beater. Melt the butter with the cocoa, cola, and coffee granules in a small saucepan over low heat. Allow to cool slightly, then drizzle the cocoa mixture into the dry ingredients with the mixer running on a slow speed, and mix until combined.

3 Add the milk, egg, and vanilla extract and mix thoroughly. Pour into the prepared pan and bake for 40 minutes. Allow to cool in the pan for 15 minutes before turning out onto a wire rack.

4 To make the topping, simply combine the ingredients in a saucepan and melt over medium heat, beating the mixture to remove any lumps. Bring to a boil and simmer for 5 minutes. Allow to cool and then spread evenly over the cake. Serve immediately or leave in a cool place until served.

BANANA AND SUNFLOWER BREAD

This seed bread is a great way of using up over-ripe bananas. It is best eaten when lightly spread with butter and honey. If covered, it will keep well for several days. It also freezes wonderfully.

MAKES 1 LARGE LOAF CAKE
PREPARATION TIME: 20 minutes
COOKING TIME: 1¼ hours

1 Preheat the oven to 350°F. Grease and line the base of a large loaf pan with wax paper.

2 Break the bananas into rough chunks in the mixer bowl and beat them into a purée using the flat beater at a medium speed. Add the eggs, vanilla extract, and butter and beat again until well mixed.

3 Add the flour, baking powder, salt, spice, sugar, and seeds to the bowl and mix well.

4 Pour the mixture into the prepared pan and sprinkle with the reserved seeds. Bake for one hour and 15 minutes or until a skewer inserted into the cake comes out clean. If the cake starts to become too brown, cover with aluminum foil or wax paper and continue cooking. Allow to cool in the pan for 10 minutes before turning out onto a wire rack to cool completely.

4 ripe bananas
2 eggs
1 tsp vanilla extract
5 oz (1¼ sticks) butter, softened
2 cups all-purpose flour, sifted
2 tsp baking powder
½ tsp salt
1 tsp pumpkin spice
⅔ cup superfine sugar
½ cup sunflower seeds, with a few reserved for garnish

ROCK BUNS

MAKES 12
PREPARATION TIME: 15 minutes
COOKING TIME: 25 to 30 minutes

¼ lb (1 stick) butter, cut into small pieces
2 cups self-rising flour
Pinch of salt
1 tsp pumpkin spice
½ cup raw sugar
1 cup mixed dried cake fruit, such as currants, raisins, sultanas, and chopped peel
1 egg, beaten
Milk to mix
Raw sugar

Sometimes the simplest recipes are the best! These have always been a strong favorite with both of us — and our families.

1 Preheat the oven to 400°F. Lightly butter a 12-hole muffin pan.
2 Blend the butter into the flour, salt, and spice using the flat beater until the mixture resembles fine breadcrumbs. Add the sugar and fruit and mix again, then add the egg and just enough milk to make a really firm dough.
3 Scoop the mixture into the prepared pan, leaving the buns roughly shaped on top. Scatter a little extra sugar over each one and bake for 25 to 30 minutes, until golden brown and set.
4 Cool on a wire rack before serving.

VIENNESE SHORTBREADS

MAKES ABOUT 20
PREPARATION TIME: 15 minutes
COOKING TIME: 10 minutes

6 oz (1½ sticks) butter
5 Tbsp confectioners' sugar
1 cup all-purpose flour, sifted
Pinch of salt
Chocolate chips, chopped candied cherries, or candied ginger for topping

Meltingly buttery, these shortbreads look professional because they are piped onto the cookie sheet — but they are so simple to do. Chocolate chips are our favorite topping, but candied cherries or candied ginger are delicious, too.

1 Preheat the oven to 400°F. Lightly butter two cookie sheets.
2 Cream the butter and sugar together until light and fluffy using the flat beater; start on a slow speed and get slightly faster. Beat in the flour and the salt, adding it in three batches, and beating well after each addition until the mixture is smooth. Continue beating until the mixture is soft enough to pipe through a pastry bag.
3 Using a pastry bag with a large star nozzle tip, pipe the mixture onto the cookie sheets in small rosette shapes. Top with chocolate chips or the topping of your choice.
4 Bake for about 10 minutes, until just set and very lightly golden. Do not allow the shortbreads to brown.
5 Cool on a wire tray.

TRADITIONAL JELLY ROLL

SERVES 6 TO 8
PREPARATION TIME: 40 minutes
COOKING TIME: 8 to 10
minutes

3 eggs, at room temperature
¾ cup superfine sugar
1 tsp vanilla extract
1 cup plus 1 Tbsp all-purpose
flour, sifted
3 to 4 Tbsp strawberry jam or
jelly
Confectioners' sugar for
dusting

It is so easy to make a jelly roll with your mixer because it does all the hard work for you. This recipe is certainly best eaten on the day it is made and can be filled with the preserves of your choice — strawberry jam is still our favorite!

1 Preheat the oven to 425°F. Line a jelly-roll pan with wax paper.

2 Whisk the eggs and sugar together until the mixture is pale and thick and leaves a trail when you lift out the wire whip. This will take 10 minutes or more. Add the vanilla extract and whisk again.

3 Sift the flour into the mixture, add the extract, and fold in lightly using a metal spoon. Pour into the prepared pan and spread lightly into the corners to level out the mixture. Bake for 8 to 10 minutes or until just firm to the touch.

4 Sprinkle superfine sugar over a large piece of wax paper on a wire rack and turn the cake out onto it. Peel the baked lining paper off the cake and trim the edges with a sharp knife. Roll the cake and wax paper up together in a tight roll and leave to cool.

5 When cool, unroll the cake and spread it with the strawberry jam, leaving a 1-inch gap around the edges. Roll the cake again, this time without the paper! Dust with sifted confectioners' sugar and cut into thick slices to serve.

HONEY AND APPLE MUESLI SQUARES

These bars are so quick and easy to make, and go really well with a cup of tea. The cornmeal adds some bite to the mixture and the honey and apple provide natural sweetness. These bars seem positively healthy!

....

1 Preheat the oven to 375°F. Grease a 9-inch square baking pan.

2 Place the flours and confectioners' sugar in the mixer bowl, add the cornmeal and the muesli, and combine using the flat beater. Add the butter and blend on a medium setting until the mixture resembles breadcrumbs. Add enough cold water (probably only about 1 to 2 tablespoons) to bind the mixture together while still retaining a crumbly appearance.

3 Press two-thirds of the mixture into the prepared pan and pack it down firmly. Drizzle the honey over this base followed by the apple in an even layer. Crumble the remaining mixture over the top and press down very lightly. Bake for about 30 minutes or until golden in color. Remove from the oven and cut immediately into bars.

4 Allow to cool completely in the pan. Store in an airtight container.

**MAKES ABOUT 16 TO 20
  SQUARES**
PREPARATION TIME: 15 minutes
COOKING TIME: 30 minutes

1⅓ cups wholewheat flour
¼ cup all-purpose flour
⅓ cup confectioners' sugar,
  sifted
⅓ cup cornmeal or instant
  polenta
¾ cup muesli or granola
½ lb (2 sticks) butter, chilled
  and diced
Cold water to mix
3 Tbsp honey
2 dessert apples, peeled,
  cored, and grated

LEMONADE SCONES

This is an amazing recipe given to us by an Australian cousin named Marlene. From the minimal list of ingredients, it's hard to imagine the perfect light and tasty end product. This quantity makes a large batch of scones but they freeze well and rarely last long anyway!

MAKES 20 TO 25 SCONES
PREPARATION TIME: 15 minutes
COOKING TIME: 10 to 15 minutes

6 cups self-rising flour
12-oz can lemonade
1 cup heavy cream
¼ tsp salt
Milk for topping (optional)

1 Preheat the oven to 400°F. Grease and flour one or two large cookie sheets.

2 Sift the flour into the mixer bowl, add the remaining ingredients, and blend using the dough hook on the slowest possible setting. It is essential that this step is carried out at the slowest speed to obtain the correct consistency of dough.

3 Turn the dough out onto a lightly floured surface. The dough will be light and fluffy and will need only a gentle helping hand to pat it out to about a ¾-inch thickness.

4 Cut into rounds with a 2-inch cookie or biscuit cutter that's been dipped in flour, or cut into triangles with a sharp knife. Place on the cookie sheet, brush with a little milk if you wish, and bake towards the top of the oven for 10 to 15 minutes, or until well risen and lightly golden.

5 Transfer to a wire rack to cool. Serve split and buttered with jam and plenty of whipped cream.

COOK'S TIP: Use the lemonade at room temperature for the best results. The dough hook is the right attachment for this recipe – it's not a mistake!

DOUBLE CHOCOLATE AND ROASTED HAZELNUT BROWNIES

MAKES ABOUT 20 SQUARES
PREPARATION TIME: 20 minutes
COOKING TIME: 30 minutes

10½ oz luxury dark chocolate

½ lb (2 sticks) butter

1 cup superfine sugar

3 eggs

2 Tbsp Frangelico liqueur (for grown-ups!)

½ cup self-rising flour

¾ cup roasted hazelnuts, chopped

½ cup white chocolate chips

This sumptuous brownie recipe is wonderfully chocolaty, and the addition of the roasted hazelnuts gives it a delicious crunch. Cut into small squares for a snack, or serve in larger pieces with ice cream and a drizzle of melted chocolate for dessert – or as a meal in itself!!

1 Preheat the oven to 375°F. Grease and line the base of a 9-inch square baking pan with wax paper.

2 Melt the chocolate with the butter (we usually use the microwave to do this; it takes about two minutes on high. The chocolate will not look melted, but stir thoroughly and you will see that this is not the case).

3 Beat the sugar and eggs thoroughly using the flat beater, then with the motor still running, gradually drizzle in the melted chocolate mixture and the Frangelico if you are using it. Allow to cool slightly, and then add the flour and hazelnuts, and mix to combine. Finally, add the white chocolate chips and fold in briefly on the lowest setting.

4 Pour the mixture into the prepared pan and bake for about 25 to 30 minutes or until just set. Remove from the oven and allow to cool in the pan. Cut into brownie-sized squares, or big ones if you're a real chocoholic!

APRICOT AND BUTTERMILK MUFFINS

These muffins couldn't be easier to make and are seriously tasty hot or cold – split them open and eat with a pat of butter or add some whipped cream! You can adapt the recipe by swapping the apricots for another dried fruit (dried cranberries are a real success) or by adding spices such as ginger or cinnamon.

1 Preheat the oven to 400°F. Line a 12-hole muffin pan with paper liners.

2 Combine the dry ingredients and mix thoroughly. Set aside.

3 Combine the remaining ingredients using the flat beater. Pour the dry ingredients into the mixer bowl and blend on the slowest speed setting. Do not beat the mixture; just fold together and do not worry about leaving lumps.

4 Using a small ladle or a ½-cup measure, fill each muffin paper about three-quarter full. Bake for about 20 to 25 minutes until firm and golden. Serve hot or cold.

COOK'S TIP: You can chop the apricots using the coarse shredding cone of the Rotor Slicer/Shredder. If you are unable to buy buttermilk, simply sour regular milk with 1 teaspoon lemon juice and allow to stand for 15 minutes at room temperature before using.

MAKES ABOUT 12 LARGE MUFFINS
PREPARATION TIME: 15 minutes
COOKING TIME: 25 to 30 minutes

2 cups all-purpose flour, sifted
1 Tbsp baking powder
½ tsp salt
¼ cup sugar
1 Tbsp grated orange zest
½ cup dried apricots, finely chopped
1 cup buttermilk
⅓ cup melted butter
1 egg, beaten

STICKY DATE AND COCONUT SLICES

MAKES ABOUT 8 TO 10 SLICES
PREPARATION TIME: 10 minutes
COOKING TIME: 30 minutes

¼ lb (1 stick) butter
1 Tbsp light corn syrup, or
    golden syrup if available
1 egg, beaten
1 cup chopped dates
1 cup raw sugar
1 cup dried flaked coconut
1 cup self-rising flour

This recipe is from a restaurant in New Zealand, which offers an amazing array of slices, bars, and pancakes. These are a particular favorite, and are wonderfully sweet and sticky to eat!

1 Preheat the oven to 325°F. Grease a 7-inch square baking pan.

2 Melt the butter and syrup together in a saucepan and then allow to cool slightly, for about five minutes.

3 In the mixer bowl combine all the dry ingredients, then add the melted mixture and the egg, and mix thoroughly using the flat beater. Pour the mixture into the pan and press down evenly.

4 Bake for about 30 minutes or until well risen and golden. The cake will be slightly soft in the center, but will become firm when cool. Cool in the pan before cutting into slices

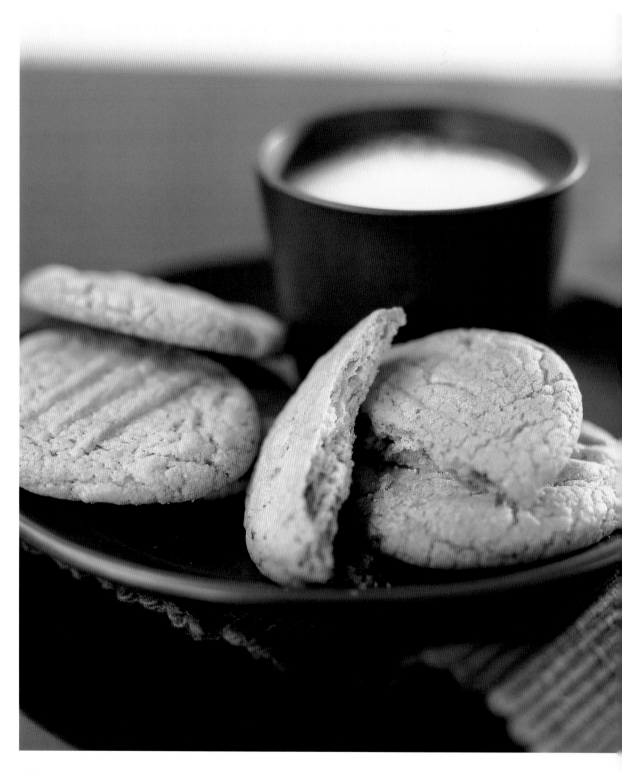

COFFEE CRUNCH COOKIES

These cookies are really light and crisp – they often spread into strange shapes in the oven, but maybe that is part of their attraction.

....

1 Preheat the oven to 400°F. Lightly grease two cookie sheets. Sift together the flour and baking powder.

2 Heat the butter slowly until melted, then simmer it for five minutes. Combine the sugar and coffee in the mixer bowl, add the hot butter, mix briefly with the flat beater, and then leave to cool for five minutes.

3 Add the egg and beat until thick and creamy, then gradually work in the flour to make a soft and shiny yet manageable dough.

4 Roll the mixture into walnut-sized pieces in your hands, place on the prepared cookie sheets, and flatten lightly with a fork. Allow plenty of room for the cookies to spread, but if they join up in the oven you can break them apart later.

5 Bake for 12 to15 minutes, until golden brown. Allow to cool slightly on the pans before transferring to a wire rack to cool completely and to become crisp.

....

COOK'S TIP: Once the cookies are completely cold, store in an airtight container.

MAKES ABOUT 30 COOKIES
PREPARATION TIME: 20 minutes
COOKING TIME: 12 to 15 minutes

2½ cups all-purpose flour
2 tsp baking powder
½ lb (2 sticks) unsalted butter
1 cup superfine sugar
2 Tbsp freeze-dried instant coffee granules
1 egg, beaten
Superfine sugar for dredging (optional)

BREADS AND BUNS

Homemade bread offers so much more in the way of flavor and texture than store bought bread, especially when purchased from supermarkets and convenience stores. We both prefer to use fresh yeast but it is not always available, so for convenience, we have created all these recipes for active dry yeast. A big advantage to this is that these doughs require just one rising period, making the whole preparation and baking time much shorter.

TOMATO AND OLIVE OIL BREAD

MAKES I LARGE LOAF
PREPARATION TIME: 3 hours,
    including rising
COOKING TIME: 25 to 30
    minutes

4 cups bread flour
I Tbsp salt
I heaped Tbsp active
    dry yeast
½ cup olive oil
I½ cups lukewarm water
12 cherry or grape tomatoes,
    halved
I to 2 cloves garlic, very finely
    sliced
Olive oil and coarse sea salt
    for topping

*Much faster to prepare than a traditional focaccia, this olive oil bread is
enlivened with sweet cherry tomatoes and a little fresh garlic. It's delicious
served with soft fresh goat cheese and a salad.*

I Blend the flour, salt, and yeast together on a low speed using the dough hook,
then add the olive oil and most of the water. Mix, and knead thoroughly on a
low speed, adding enough water to make a soft but manageable dough. The
kneading will take about four to six minutes.

2 Scrape the dough off the hook back into the bowl. Cover with plastic wrap
and leave in a warm place for two hours until well risen.

3 Return the bowl to the mixer and knead the dough again to its original size
with the dough hook on speed 2. Turn out onto a lightly floured surface.

4 Generously oil a small rectangular roasting pan (about 8 x 10 inches). Divide
the dough in half, and roll out one piece to roughly fit the base of the pan,
stretching it into the corners. Cover with the halved tomatoes and garlic and
season lightly with salt and pepper. Roll out the remaining dough and place it
over the tomatoes. Cover the pan with plastic wrap and leave in a warm place
again for about 20 minutes, until just starting to rise.

5 Preheat the oven to 425°F. Carefully make indentations all over the dough
with your fingertips; this will seal the two halves together and stop the dough
from rising too much. Drizzle with a little olive oil and sprinkle with coarse sea
salt, then bake for 25 to 30 minutes, until golden brown.

6 Cool on a wire rack before serving.

RUSTIC OLIVE BREAD

Here is a country-style bread, heavy with the oil and fruits of the olive. The richness of the dough means that it is slow to rise, but the flavor is fabulous. Ensure that the olives are well drained before adding them to the dough, or the bread will become heavy and difficult to handle. Use stuffed olives if you like – those with jalapeno peppers are especially good.

MAKES I LARGE LOAF
PREPARATION TIME: 2 hours,
   including rising
COOKING TIME: 30 minutes

4 cups bread flour
I tsp salt
I Tbsp active dry yeast
½ cup good quality extra
   virgin olive oil
About I½ cups lukewarm
   water
I cup pitted green olives,
   roughly chopped

I Blend the flour, salt, and yeast together in the mixer bowl with the dough hook, then add the oil and most of the water. Mix to a manageable dough, adding more water if necessary, and knead thoroughly for at least four minutes.
2 Add the olives to the dough and work them in gently on a very slow speed.
3 Turn the dough out onto a lightly floured surface and shape into a round loaf, and then place on an oiled cookie sheet. Cover and leave in a warm place to rise for one to one and a half hours, until doubled in size.
4 Preheat the oven to 425°F. Brush the loaf with a little extra olive oil if you wish. Bake for 30 minutes, until the base sounds hollow when tapped and the loaf is lightly golden. Cool on a wire rack and break into rough chunks to serve.

LIGHT RYE BREAD

MAKES I LOAF

PREPARATION TIME: I½ hours, including rising

COOKING TIME: 35 to 40 minutes

2 cups bread flour

2 cups rye flour

2 tsp salt

I heaped Tbsp active dry yeast

3 Tbsp olive oil

About 2 cups warm water

This is a basic bread recipe that can be used for almost any flour – vary the quantities of white and wholewheat or rye flour as you wish. Use the same method for an all-white bread, too. For this rye loaf, we have used half rye and half white flour, giving a moist crumb with a crispy crust.

I Mix the flours, salt, and yeast in the mixer bowl, then add the oil and most of the water. Mix to a manageable dough using the dough hook, adding a little more water if necessary. Knead thoroughly for four to six minutes until smooth.

2 Shape the dough on a lightly floured surface into a round loaf and place on an oiled cookie sheet. Cover and leave in a warm place to rise for about one hour, until doubled in size.

3 Preheat the oven to 425°F. Scatter a little more flour (rye or white) over the loaf, and bake for 35 to 40 minutes. The crust should be well browned and the base of the loaf will sound hollow when tapped. Cool on a wire rack.

BARA BRITH

This richly fruited sweet loaf is a traditional recipe from Wales, and is often served sliced with butter for an afternoon snack. It is slow to rise because it contains a great deal of fruit, which is worked into the dough after the main kneading to preserve the color of the bread's crumb. This can be a real effort to make by hand and is much easier with the mixer.

1 Blend the butter into the flour and salt using the flat beater, then add the sugar, spice, and yeast and blend again.

2 Add the egg and water and mix to a soft but not sticky dough using the dough hook. Knead for about four minutes until smooth, adding a little more water if necessary.

3 Gradually knead in the fruit using the dough hook; it may be necessary to turn the dough over in the fruit in the bowl once or twice by hand during this process as the fruit may collect under the dough.

4 Turn out onto a lightly floured surface and gently shape into a smooth round; try to make sure that all the fruit on the top is coated in dough, even just very thinly, as this will stop the fruit from burning in the oven. Place the loaf on a greased cookie sheet, cover, and leave in a warm place for two hours or even longer, until well risen.

5 Preheat the oven to 350°F. Brush the loaf with milk or a little beaten egg, dredge lightly with sugar, and then bake for 35 to 40 minutes, until golden brown. (The Bara Brith is a bit too rich to really sound hollow when tapped on the base, so don't use it as a test for doneness.)

6 Cool on a wire rack. Serve sliced and buttered.

MAKES I LARGE LOAF
PREPARATION TIME: 2 to 2½ hours, including rising
COOKING TIME: 35 to 40 minutes

2 oz (½ stick) butter
3 cups bread flour
I tsp salt
2 Tbsp superfine sugar
½ tsp pumpkin pie spice
I heaped Tbsp active dry yeast
I egg, beaten
⅔ cup lukewarm water
2 cups mixed dried fruit, such as currants, raisins, sultanas, and chopped peel
Milk or beaten egg and superfine sugar for topping

STOLLEN

MAKES 2 LOAVES

PREPARATION TIME: about 2 hours, including rising

COOKING TIME: 30 minutes

I heaped Tbsp active
   dry yeast

I tsp superfine sugar

4 cups all-purpose flour

⅔ cup lukewarm milk

Pinch of salt

3 Tbsp light brown sugar, or
   light Muscovado sugar if
   available

2 oz (½ stick) butter, cut into
   slices, plus a little extra for
   finishing

2 eggs, beaten

I Tbsp rum

I cup mixed dried fruit, such
   as currants, raisins, sultanas,
   and chopped peel

Grated rind of half a lemon

7-oz tube prepared marzipan
   or almond paste

Confectioners' sugar for
   topping

These traditional Christmas loaves are found all over northern Europe, although they originally hail from Germany. The secret of a successful marzipan-filled stollen is not to place the marzipan right on the fold of the bread, or it may well spring open during rising or baking. Tie with a ribbon to make a tasty gift for friends. All-purpose flour is used so that the stollen are not too light and doughy.

1 Blend the yeast, superfine sugar, 1 cup of flour, and the milk together in the mixer bowl. Cover and leave in a warm place for at least an hour, until it starts to become frothy.

2 Add the remaining flour, salt, brown sugar, butter, most (not all!) of the beaten eggs, and the rum, and mix to a manageable dough with the dough hook, adding a little extra milk if necessary. Knead thoroughly for about four minutes, then cover and leave in a warm place for an hour, or until doubled in size.

3 Knead the dough lightly, then gently work in the dried fruit and lemon rind using the dough hook. Do not over knead. Turn out onto a lightly floured surface and divide into two. Shape into ovals, a half-inch thick.

4 Roll the marzipan into two even lengths to fit the length of the stollen. Press the rolling pin into the dough to make an indentation about one-third of the way from the bottom of each oval. Lay the marzipan in the marked places then fold the dough over towards you, leaving the ends of the marzipan just showing if possible. Seal the edges with some of the remaining beaten egg. Place the stollens on a lightly buttered cookie sheet, cover, and leave to rise again for about 30 minutes.

5 Preheat the oven to 350°F. Brush the dough with any remaining egg and bake for 30 minutes, or until golden brown.

6 Cool on a wire rack. Melt a little extra butter and brush over the cooled stollens, and then top with sifted confectioners' sugar.

SPANISH-STYLE SEEDED LOAF

This olive oil bread is heavy with toasted nuts and seeds — it's fabulous with soup, cheeses, or spicy meats like chorizo sausage. We usually don't add the extras until we have kneaded the dough, but in this case, it is actually a good thing to really knead them into the dough because it allows the nuts and seeds to break up a little.

1 Toast the hazelnuts and pine nuts until golden brown, either in a dry skillet or under the broiler. Cool slightly, then place in the mixer bowl with the remaining dry ingredients. Add the oil and most of the water, then mix to a pliable, manageable dough using the dough hook. Add extra water if necessary, but feel the dough first.

2 Knead thoroughly for about four to six minutes on a slow speed.

3 Turn out onto a floured surface and lightly knead the dough by hand until smooth, then shape into a round loaf. Place on an oiled cookie sheet and leave to rise in a warm place for about one hour, until doubled in size.

4 Preheat the oven to 425°F. Dust the loaf lightly with flour and then bake for 30 to 35 minutes, or until the base sounds hollow when tapped. Cool before eating.

MAKES 1 LARGE LOAF
PREPARATION TIME: 1 hour 15 minutes, including rising
COOKING TIME: 30 to 35 minutes

⅓ **cup hazelnuts, roughly chopped**
2 **Tbsp pine nuts**
4 **cups bread flour**
1 **tsp salt**
⅓ **cup pumpkin seeds, or pumpkin and sunflower seeds mixed**
2 **Tbsp sesame seeds**
1 **Tbsp active dry yeast**
5 **Tbsp extra virgin olive oil**
1 **to 1¼ cups lukewarm water**

APPLE AND CINNAMON DOUGHNUTS

MAKES 8
PREPARATION TIME : 1¾ hours
COOKING TIME : about 10 minutes

2 cups all-purpose flour
½ tsp salt
2 tsp active dry yeast
1 Tbsp sunflower or vegetable oil
1 egg, beaten
⅔ cup warm water
1 dessert apple, peeled and diced
Oil for deep-frying
Superfine sugar and ground cinnamon for coating

Homemade doughnuts just have to be one of the most fun and special things we make! These days, you can get jam in a squirt bottle, which could be used to fill the doughnuts, but we salve our consciences by making apple doughnuts, thinking that the fruit will be good for us!

1 Mix the flour, salt, and yeast together in the mixer bowl, then add the oil, egg, and most of the water. Mix to a manageable dough with the dough hook, adding a little more water if necessary, then knead thoroughly for four to six minutes until smooth and elastic. Cover the bowl and leave in a warm place to rise for about one hour, until doubled in size.

2 Cut eight small squares of wax paper, and bring a large pan of water to a boil. Knead the dough again lightly with the dough hook, then turn out onto a lightly floured surface and divide into eight pieces. Knead each piece until smooth and form into discs. Place a little of the apple on each one and shape the dough around it, pinching the edges together to seal. Place each doughnut on a piece of wax paper, sealed side down, and leave for 10 minutes.

3 Heat the oil for frying until it reaches 360°F on a thermometer inserted in the oil. Lift the doughnuts with the paper, to avoid causing the risen dough to fall back. Blanch the doughnuts in the boiling water for just a few seconds; the paper will float off and you can skim it out of the pan. Remove the doughnuts with a slotted spoon and drain on crumpled paper towels.

4 Fry the doughnuts in the oil for six to eight minutes, turning once, until golden brown. They will "grow" during cooking, so cook no more than four at a time. Drain on paper towels and then toss in the sugar and cinnamon. Allow to cool before eating.

ZUCCHINI ROLLS

This recipe yields a moist white bread, which is perfect with soups, cheeses, and cold meats. Shred the zucchini with the Rotor Slicer/Shredder, and squeeze as much moisture out as possible before salting. This is a necessary process and not just a whim; otherwise, the dough becomes too wet during kneading and is very difficult to handle.

MAKES 8
PREPARATION TIME: 2½ hours,
   including salting and rising
COOKING TIME: 30 minutes

⅓ lb zucchini, trimmed (about
   2 medium zucchinis)
Salt (see method)
3 cups bread flour
1 tsp salt
1 Tbsp active dry yeast
**1 Tbsp sunflower or vegetable
   oil**
About 1 cup warm water
Beaten egg for glazing

1 Shred the zucchini coarsely using the Rotor Slicer/Shredder; catch it in a clean dish towel placed over the mixer bowl, and then wrapping the zucchini in the cloth, squeeze out as much water as possible. Place the zucchini in a colander, sprinkle generously with salt, and leave for one hour. Rinse thoroughly with cold water, and then squeeze dry again in your hands.

2 Mix the zucchini with the flour, measured salt, and yeast in the mixer bowl, then add the oil and most of the water. Mix to a dough with the dough hook; the dough should be a bit drier than usual to allow for any extra juices coming out of the zucchini during kneading. Knead for five to six minutes, adding a little extra water if necessary.

3 Divide the dough into eight pieces and shape into rolls, placing them in an oiled 10-inch round springform pan. Cover and leave in a warm place to rise for about an hour.

4 Preheat the oven to 425°F. Brush the top of the rolls with a little beaten egg – decadent yes, but it gives a soft yet wonderfully golden crust – and bake for 30 minutes. Remove from the pan, cool, and tear apart to eat.

MORNING ROLLS

MAKES 12

PREPARATION TIME: overnight rising, plus 45 minutes

COOKING TIME: 20 to 25 minutes

FOR THE OVERNIGHT DOUGH:
3 cups all-purpose flour
2 tsp salt
1 Tbsp active dry yeast, divided (use 1 tsp and save the rest)
2 cups cold water

FOR THE MORNING DOUGH:
½ cup warm water
4 cups all-purpose flour
2 oz (½ stick) butter, cut into small pieces
1 tsp superfine sugar

Start the first dough just as you go to bed, then get up early the next day to finish the mixing and to shape the rolls. It really is worth the effort, especially when you have guests staying overnight. The long rising time gives the rolls a soft, creamy texture and a real depth of flavor.

1 Make the overnight dough, starting just before bed the night before you want to serve them. Place the flour, salt, and 1 teaspoon yeast in the bowl, add the water and just combine to make a lumpy dough. Cover the bowl with plastic wrap and leave in the kitchen until morning.

2 The next day, make the morning dough. To the same bowl with the overnight dough, add the water, flour, butter, sugar, and the remaining yeast. Mix thoroughly using the dough hook, and then knead for about six minutes, until the dough is smooth and elastic.

3 On a lightly floured surface, shape the dough into 12 rolls and place on an oiled jelly-roll pan. Cover and leave for 30 minutes in a warm place.

4 Preheat the oven to 400°F. Bake the rolls for 20 to 25 minutes, until lightly golden. The rolls should look cooked on the base; they will not be crusty enough to really sound hollow when tapped.

CHELSEA BUNS

Although we have used active dry yeast for these delicious fruited buns, we have still given the dough two full rising periods, plus an extra fermentation for the yeast at the beginning. This ensures a really light result with a good creamy texture and flavor. We like icing on our buns, so we've included that too!

MAKES 8
PREPARATION TIME: 2½ to 3 hours, including rising
COOKING TIME: 30 to 35 minutes

2 cups bread flour
1 heaped Tbsp active dry yeast
½ cup lukewarm milk
½ tsp salt
2 oz (½ stick) butter
1 egg, beaten
⅔ cup mixed dried fruit, such as currants, raisins, sultanas, and chopped peel
⅓ cup light brown sugar, or light Muscovado sugar if available
⅔ cup confectioners' sugar, sifted

1 Place ½ cup flour in a bowl with the yeast and milk, cover, and leave in a warm place for 30 minutes or until it begins to slowly ferment.

2 Mix the salt with the remaining flour in the mixer bowl, add half the butter, and blend it in using the flat beater. Add the yeast mixture and the egg and mix to a soft dough using the dough hook; add a little more milk or water if necessary. Knead thoroughly to make a soft, ever so slightly sticky dough that leaves the sides of the bowl easily during kneading. Continue to knead for five minutes on a low to medium speed.

3 Cover the bowl and leave in a warm place for about an hour and a half, until the dough is well risen and has doubled in size. Knead gently again using the dough hook. Melt the remaining butter and allow it to cool.

4 Roll the dough out on a lightly floured surface to a rectangle about 12 x 8 inches. Turn the dough around after each rolling and pull out the corners with your fingers to keep the rectangular shape.

5 Brush the dough generously with most of the melted butter, then use the remainder to grease a 10-inch round springform pan. Mix the fruit with the brown sugar and sprinkle it evenly over the dough before rolling up from one of the long sides. Cut the dough into eight slices and arrange them in the prepared pan.

6 Cover the pan again and leave for another 30 minutes, until the buns have risen and are puffy and start to spread towards each other.

7 Preheat the oven to 375°F and bake the buns for 30 to 35 minutes. Allow to cool slightly in the pan.

8 Blend the confectioners' sugar with a little water, then drizzle it over the warm buns. Leave to set before removing the buns from the pan, breaking them apart. Serve buttered if you are feeling very decadent!

INDEX

ACKNOWLEDGMENTS

Mixers have been a part of my life for as long as I have been making a living, in one way or another, with food. So many thanks to the TDA Test Kitchen, and especially to Val Collins, my first boss. Also to Linda Kirk and all the Kenwood team, at home and all around the world, who taught me so much.

A big Thank You to Claire Small, who tested some of the recipes on work experience from school and was the most enormous help. Your constructive comments were greatly appreciated and good luck in finding a cooking career - you'll be fabulous!

Special thanks to my husband Nick who has eaten every single one of my recipes in this and countless other books, and remains just one trouser size larger than when we married 21 years ago! And to all my friends and colleagues who bake and keep the art of home cooking alive.

ROSEMARY MOON

My thanks go to the marvellous Mrs Moon for making this, and so much else, possible; and to Anna and Peta for setting me off in the first place! A big mention to my Ozzie support team who have inspired me throughout the planning and writing of this book – your friendship, kindness, and ability to be completely silly, will never be forgotten – Scotty and Dominico in Dubbo; the Team at Café Café, Subiaco; Dennis and Scarlet in Noggerup. Most importantly to my Australian family – The Foodies Extraordinaire at Starlings; and champion cake maker Mummy Marlene.

To my darling Daddy and my wonderful brother Si, who between them, bravely ate their way through each recipe test without complaint, and to my Mum who encouraged me to bake my first cake and has encouraged me ever since.

KATIE BISHOP

The Publisher would like to thank the team at Wild Card Public Relations, especially Jen Eveleigh, for help with the loan of KitchenAid mixers.

KitchenAid mixers can be bought across the world.
Visit the website at www.kitchenAid.com.

Customer service centers:

USA:
P.O.Box 218
St. Joseph
MI 49085
1-800-541-6390

Europe:
KitchenAid Europa
Nijverheidslaan
3-Box 5
B-1853
Strombeek-Bever
Belgium

UK:
CAD
Apuro Ltd
Unit 21A
Monkspath Business Park
Solihull, B90 4NZ
0845 450 0099

Australia:
55 Broadmeadow Road
Broadmeadow NSW 2298
Help Desk phone line: 1800 990 990

When using the grinder and sausage stuffer to make sausages, natural casings are required. These can be mail-ordered from:

International Casings Group
4420 S.Woolcott,
Chicago,
IL 60609, USA
www.casings.com

or

Spicetech UK,
Whaley Bridge,
Derbyshire SK23 7AZ
www.spicetech.co.uk